HENRY COTTON'S
GUIDE TO
GOLF IN THE BRITISH ISLES

CLIVEDEN PRESS

Contents

INTRODUCTION

Early golf courses were wholly natural: rabbits and sheep were the only greenkeepers, and no boundaries separated the course from Farmer Brown's sheep or prevented its use as a playground by any neighbouring children. On these first crude courses all distinctions of rank were levelled in the enjoyment of the game as the lords of the land swung clubs with the artisans and peasants.

The middle of the eighteenth century saw the formation of the first golf clubs and, with them, the beginning of the modern history of golf. Many of the old courses were so well designed originally that they have survived almost unchanged; others have been modernised to provide an adequate test for the present standard of golf.

The British Isles abound in all sorts of beautiful golfing country. There are seaside courses and inland courses; clubs which are attached to luxurious hotels and others so steeped in the history of the game that they have become places of pilgrimage to golfers from all over the world.

From these vast number of courses dotting our isles I have chosen a random but representative selection. Some of these are familiar ground to me, scenes of personal triumph or disappointment, others I have played occasionally and enjoyed. But they are all great courses . . . so take your pick, and good golfing!

Wentworth Golf Club

Virginia Water, Surrey

Tel: Wentworth 2201

Secretary: Air Commodore F. A. Pearce
Tel: Wentworth 2202

Nearest station: Virginia Water, 1½ miles

Hotels: Great Fosters, Egham;
Royal Forrèsters Hotel, Ascot

Course records: East Course
Professional, 63 by A. Miguel
Amateur, 65 by G. B. Wolstenholme
West Course
Professional, 65 by N. C. Coles
Amateur, 70 by J. Povall

Visitors' fees: Weekdays 42/— per day or
introduction by a member is necessary
No visitors at weekends unless playing
with member

West Course **18 holes, 6997 yards**
East Course **18 holes, 6202 yards**

	West yards	East yards		West yards	East yards
1st hole	476	386	10th hole	190	183
2nd hole	157	425	11th hole	408	478
3rd hole	457	333	12th hole	480	158
4th hole	497	195	13th hole	437	397
5th hole	192	330	14th hole	183	305
6th hole	347	360	15th hole	480	350
7th hole	403	228	16th hole	380	467
8th hole	400	442	17th hole	555	217
9th hole	460	525	18th hole	495	423

Nicknames for individual holes and hazards are quite common in golf, but I know of only one course which has gained its own pet name. That is the West Course at Wentworth, which has been affectionately named the 'Burma Road' by the professionals. This course is a great test of golf of international calibre.

Wentworth, complete with swimming pool, tennis courts and ballroom, is one of Britain's few country clubs in the American style, but it is for the golf that it is principally known. Designed by Harry Colt, the courses are carved out of that heather, fir, rhododendron and silver birch country which lends itself to the best of inland golf.

The clubhouse, one of the most beautiful in England, was previously the home of the Spanish Countess Morella. It stands about a mile and a half from Virginia Water station on the southern electric line from Waterloo.

In the dry summer of 1927, with no water on the greens, I played on the East Course at Wentworth in the *Daily Mail* Pro Tournament and hit the headlines because, when up with the leaders, I skated my ball to and fro across the 18th green from bunker to bunker, before the eyes of the crowd around the green, to close my round with a 9.

I held the West course record at Wentworth with a 64 from 1936 until just recently when a few yards were added to the 10th tee. The new record of 65 is held by Neil Coles.

The two par 5 closing holes on the West Course are killers with out-of-bounds on all sides of them, and players often make or break their rounds here. I remember, finishing with three 3s in a tournament before the war – a birdie and two eagles in a row!

Tom Haliburton, professional, writes:

Wentworth has two eighteen-hole courses and a nine-hole course. The West Course has qualities difficult to define – it is one of those courses where you don't appreciate the difficulties until you have played over it in a tournament with a card and pencil in hand. The greens are large and the short putts – those 3–6 footers – are hard to guess right when they are keen. The older East Course, though it has been the scene of many big matches and meetings, is laid out on less exacting lines, making it an ideal test for the handicap golfer.

All the courses have the same attractive woodland setting, with occasional glimpses of lake and waterfall and stream.

I think our best hole is the 7th on the West Course, a medium-length two-shotter of 403 yards. The tee is set back in an alcove of the woods at this hole. The drive is downhill into a shallow gulley fringed by bunkers on the left and right. Big hitters take an iron or lower wood to avoid running into heather at the bottom. The second shot has to be played up a steep rise over a belt of rough to a plateau double-terraced green, guarded by a deep bunker on the right.

At Wentworth we have a first-class practice ground which I run as a driving range with a man permanently in attendance.

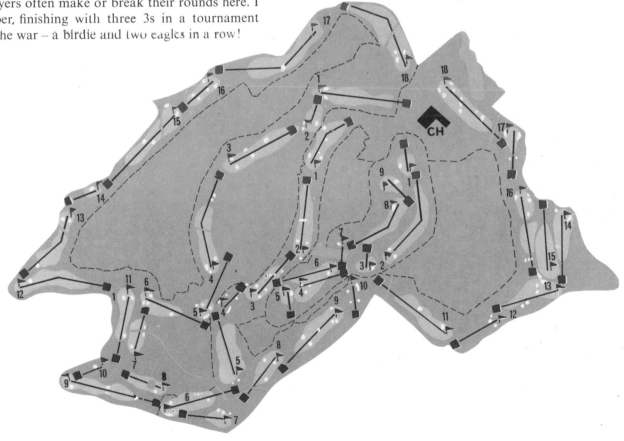

Royal Lytham St. Annes Golf Club
Links Gate, St. Annes-on-Sea, Lancashire

Tel: St. Annes 24206

Secretary: J. G. Carruthers
Tel: St. Annes 24207

Nearest station: St. Annes-on-Sea − ½ mile

Hotels: Club has Dormy accommodation and there are many hotels in the area

Visitors' fees: Weekdays 30/− per day or round (10/− with member);

Weekends 40/− (20/− with member). Visitors welcome with member or on production of introductory letter from own club

18 holes, 6670 yards

	yards		yards
1st hole	208	10th hole	336
2nd hole	426	11th hole	483
3rd hole	456	12th hole	189
4th hole	393	13th hole	339
5th hole	188	14th hole	445
6th hole	466	15th hole	462
7th hole	553	16th hole	356
8th hole	394	17th hole	423
9th hole	164	18th hole	389

One of England's great courses, both from a golfing and a traditional point of view, Royal Lytham has provided excellent golfing facilities for members and visitors since 1897. It has a long and distinguished list of events held over the sandy course with its great carries, strategic bunkers and crude rough. The course is built on nature's best golfing country, and as the railway runs along the first nine holes it pays not to cut the hole. The club also boasts a fine practice ground and putting green in ideal locations.

I think that the 483-yard 11th is the hardest hole – a blind tee shot over a row of deep bunkers cut in a sandhill crossing the narrow fairway which runs between a spinney on the left and deep rough on the right. The second shot is to a well-guarded green with some trees on the left and a wood beyond the putting surface – a real terror!

The old fashioned clubhouse has its lounge windows some five yards from the edge of the putting green of the 18th hole and there, watched from the window seats, some of golf's great dramas have been staged in the Open, the Amateur, the Ryder Cup, the Ladies' Open and some of the other big events that have been played at Lytham.

I remember playing for the first time at Royal Lytham in a professional tournament in the twenties. It was a hot summer and the greens were brown and like ice to play on. At the 9th hole, a short one of 163 yards, we had to pitch deliberately into the sand from the tee, because with the out-of-bounds beyond the green and thick rough around the green, the only chance to get a four or a three was to explode from the sand, the green could not hold the tee shot. Now the well-watered greens are almost too soft.

How Peter Thomson got round this testing course in 63 strokes is a puzzle to anyone knowing the holes and the abounding trouble. Twenty-nine has been shot going out and I think that three of the four short holes coming in the first nine make this possible. There are two hundred sandtraps on this course to be avoided, but as the course is around 6800 yards the professionals break 70 quite often in decent weather.

Royal Lytham's most famous hole is the dogleg 17th where the greatest of all American amateurs, Bobby Jones, won the first of his Open Championships in 1926. His winning shot at the 17th was so wonderful and noteworthy that it is commemorated by a brass plaque embedded in the side of the bunker. A lady visitor to the spot many years later was much impressed by this and asked in awed tones, "Is it true that Bobby Jones is buried here?"

E. T. Musty, professional, writes:

Although there are no holes here that have made the course famous from the playing point of view – such as the 'road' hole at St Andrew's – numerous stories of Lytham holes have achieved fame through the important, or sometimes amusing, part they have played in Championship battles.

The 17th is always remembered as the Bobby Jones hole, where he made the green from a pot bunker using a hickory-shafted 'Pipe' brand iron to win the 1926 Open Championship. Bobby Locke also played a really great second shot at this hole to win the Open Championship in 1952. In the same championship Fred Daly found the 11th his trouble hole, as did many others.

There are no bad holes on this course, which I consider to be the fairest all-round test of any of the championship courses, the greens being always true and consistent. I think the 8th is the hardest hole for the good player, with its elevated tee, narrow fairway below and elevated green on the ridge. From the figures I kept at the last Open Championship played here this was the only hole that players averaged more than the par 4 for the last day's play. Most handicap players tell me sad tales of the 15th hole, a long drive into the sea winds, slightly dogleg for the shorter hitter and with a narrow fairway, deep traps across at 390 yards and the green well guarded.

Some years ago a visitor with a 12 handicap took me out for a round and drove the 10th and the 18th holes, 336 and 389 yards respectively. Definitely the longest hitter I have ever seen!

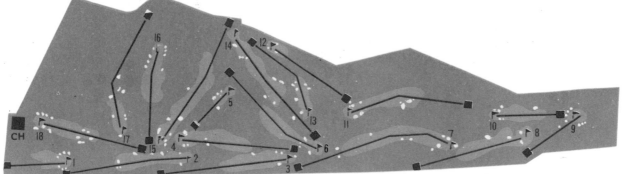

Ipswich Golf Club

Purdis Heath, Ipswich, Suffolk

Tel: Ipswich 78941

Nearest station: Ipswich – 2 miles

Hotels: Gold Lion Hotel, Ipswich;
Great White Horse Hotel, Ipswich.

Course record: Professional, 67 by R. A. Knight
Amateur, 68 by David Whinney

Visitors' fees: Weekdays 20/– per round,
30/– per day;
Weekends 30/– per round,
40/– per day.

Length of Courses:
18 and 9 holes, 6405 and 1950 yards

	yards	yards		yards
1st hole	330	105	10th hole	153
2nd hole	512	280	11th hole	531
3rd hole	163	120	12th hole	363
4th hole	425	360	13th hole	406
5th hole	433	120	14th hole	440
6th hole	182	305	15th hole	141
7th hole	437	190	16th hole	298
8th hole	373	125	17th hole	497
9th hole	308	345	18th hole	413

Here is a course set in ideal golfing country. For quietness and peace you might be a hundred miles from anywhere, yet this course is within easy access of Ipswich.

There is another great asset. Ipswich is one of the driest places in Britain, with an annual rainfall around twenty inches, so the course on Purdis Heath is always playable. It lies on undulating heathland and on sandy soil; in parts it could merit being called parkland, as many holes lie in or adjoining large spinneys.

James Braid designed this course and in 1928, at the age of twenty-one, I joined Braid with J. H. Taylor and Abe Mitchell at the opening of the course and clubhouse. The clubhouse was built as a large country house so that in case the golf project did not succeed the property could easily be sold – such was the uncertainty about the growth of golf when I came into the game!

Braid's plan was so good that the course has not been touched since we opened it. With its two starting points near the clubhouse it is undoubtedly one of Braid's happiest achievements. I think the large greens are difficult to putt on: this is shown by the professional record standing at 67 by Reg Knight, a former assistant of mine at Ashridge. Many will disagree with Phil Higgins' assessment of the 11th as the most difficult hole, but it is stroke 1 on the card.

The practice ground at Purdis Heath is small but I was proud to open a new nine-hole course there on the 40th anniversary of the opening of the major course. This helps to relieve the big course and gives beginners a chance to learn the game. My only possible criticism of the new nine-hole course is that it is too tough for most players, although great fun for a real golfer to play.

My most vivid memory of my first visit to Ipswich in 1928 is of Abe Mitchell driving the 9th green 308 yards and the uphill 16th 298 yards – and with hickory-shaped clubs and a Silver King ball!

Phil Higgins, professional, writes:

A heathland course, Ipswich is a first-class test of golf. The greens are large with gentle slopes, and as they are usually rather quick the most difficult thing here is judging the distances.

The 11th is, in my opinion, our toughest hole. It is 531 yards long and it requires a very accurate drive and even after that is achieved the second shot is narrow and blind over two cross bunkers to the green. The 5th hole of 433 yards terrifies the members. Here a long carry from the tee is essential, but the second shot off a downhill lie with a big iron or a wood is a trial.

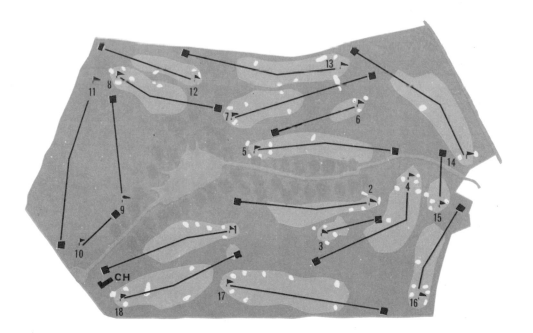

Royal Blackheath Golf Club

Court Road, Eltham, London SE9

Tel: Eltham 8479

Secretary: Major G. H. A. Yates
Tel: Eltham 1042

Nearest station: Mottingham — 10 minutes

Buses: 161, 126, 124

Hotel: Bromley Court Hotel, Bromley

Visitors' fees: Weekdays 15/— per round,
20/— per day;

Weekends and Bank Holidays,
30/— per round, 40/— per day.

Half fees if playing with member.

Course record: 66 by W. C. Thomas

18 holes, 6140 yards

	yards		yards
1st hole	465	10th hole	350
2nd hole	395	11th hole	350
3rd hole	435	12th hole	185
4th hole	195	13th hole	510
5th hole	350	14th hole	360
6th hole	470	15th hole	345
7th hole	370	16th hole	140
8th hole	160	17th hole	400
9th hole	360	18th hole	300

The Royal Blackheath Golf Club claims to be the oldest golf club in the world. Tradition has it that James VI of Scotland – James I of England – founded a Society of Golfers in 1608. It is to this society that Royal Blackheath traces its origins, although the club has moved several times in the intervening years to find a permanent home at last on the present site at Eltham.

Golf was played on the original course, a layout of 21 holes, until 1914; but in 1923 a historic decision was reached. This was to merge the ancient foundation with the Eltham Golf Club, founded in 1891.

The present park course, extending to over 100 acres, owes much to the genius of the great James Braid who redesigned it in two attractive loops around the clubhouse, creating eighteen holes of great interest, and deceptively testing too.

Over the years the golfers of Blackheath have founded, sponsored or financially assisted golf clubs the world over. The clubhouse, a fine example of later Renaissance architecture, contains many treasured golfing heirlooms, including ceremonial silver clubs with silver balls attached to them for every Field Marshal and Captain of recorded history. This famous club, situated almost in the heart of London, has played a very important part in the history of the golf game.

George Johnson, professional, writes:

This is a deceptive course: while it might seem easy at first play one soon discovers that it is not as easy as it appears to score on this course. It calls for good driving, as there are a number of slightly dogleg holes at the end of a drive, or a couple of bunkers or trees to avoid, and generally the greens are well guarded for the slightly off-shot.

I would say our best hole is the 2nd, 395 yards with an uphill second shot. It is a left to right dogleg with a bunker each side of the fairway and trees on both sides. The 300-yard 18th hole looks easy on the card, but this is a hole that cannot be bullied. I like to play short of the narrow gap in the hedge and pitch for my birdie.

My lowest score in a friendly match has been 64, but I am always pleased to keep below 70.

Walton Heath Golf Club

Tadworth, Surrey

Tel: Tadworth 2060

Secretary: Lieutenant Colonel G. P. Badham
Tel: Tadworth 2380

Nearest hotel: Burford Bridge, Dorking

Course record: Old Course, 66 by K. Bousfield
New Course, 64 by C. Clark

Visitors' fees: Weekdays 30/– (15/– with member)
Weekends 40/–

Old Course, 18 holes, 6858 yards
New Course, 18 holes, 6612 yards

	Old yards	New yards		Old yards	New yards
1st hole	310	296	10th hole	414	204
2nd hole	476	146	11th hole	190	400
3rd hole	263	423	12th hole	371	434
4th hole	453	260	13th hole	516	489
5th hole	395	470	14th hole	520	433
6th hole	400	173	15th hole	394	380
7th hole	176	396	16th hole	499	522
8th hole	457	517	17th hole	176	226
9th hole	436	458	18th hole	412	385

Some eighteen and a half miles from the West End of London and a mile from Tadworth Station are the two famous courses of Walton Heath, lying on exposed heathland, where gorse, broom, heather and bracken grow in profusion between the silver birches to make as fine a pair of natural inland courses as there are in any corner of the world. The Old Course – designed originally by Herbert Fowler – has been altered and modernised to provide a great test of golf for even the longest players.

Starting at 700 feet above sea level it can be draughty at times on this exposed heath, and if the wind is westerly then some of the heather-lined fairways are hard to hit and stay on.

There are all sorts of splendid and difficult holes at Walton Heath, but I think one of the best in the country is the 16th on the Old Course, 499 yards to an elevated green with a severe contra cross slope before it, running left to right, dragging the ball with it to a deep sand bunker.

The owner of the club, Sir William Carr, club president and chairman of the *News of the World* Organisation, is a Match Play enthusiast, and the *News of the World* P.S.A. Match Play Championship is an annual event at Walton Heath. The English Amateur Championship has also been played there, and Sir Ernest Holderness, the famous amateur golfer, is a member.

I have enjoyed dozens of rounds on Walton Heath and have had some triumphs there, even beating American Benny Shute over 72 holes in an unofficial World Title match by 6 and 5. One hole is named after me, for a tee shot I did which resulted in the match – R. A. Whitcombe and myself against Bobby Locke and Syd Breus of South Africa – turning in our favour on this very shot. I cut across the trouble at the dogleg, 345 yards 12 hole, landed just short of the green and chipped dead for a 'birdie 3'. We won by 2 and 1.

Everything about Walton Heath is first class: the clubhouse, the food, the service . . . and the golf.

Harry Busson, professional, writes:

The two Walton Heath courses are probably the best of their type in the British Isles, testing heath type courses with heather-lined fairways, situated about six hundred feet above sea level.

Our greens are large and tricky and nearly always in first class condition – we have so many societies and tournaments during the year they have to be. We have quite a good practice area.

I think all the holes are fairly tough, but the most demanding is, perhaps, the 5th on the Old Course from the back tee. The tee shot is critical and, owing to the undulating shape of the green, it is difficult to get near the pin with the second shot and three putts are common; therefore, as a par 4, I consider it difficult. Most members, however, would regard the 17th hole as the most difficult, owing to the surrounding ground being so rough. For many it is often a full wood of some sort, and if the player cannot get the distance in terms of 'carry' over the bunker, there is no area he can play for with a chance of a fair lie.

I came to Walton Heath in 1951. My predecessor was James Braid who won the News of the World *Match Play here in 1905 and was the first professional to win this tournament, at Sunningdale in 1903.*

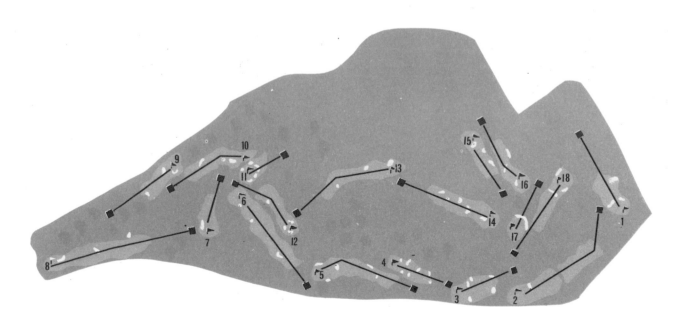

Royal St. George's Golf Club

Sandwich, Kent

Tel: Sandwich 3008

Secretary: Wing Commander H. D. Nicholson
Tel: Sandwich 3090

Nearest station: Sandwich, 1½ miles

Course record: Professional, 64 by Tony Jacklin

Visitors' fees: Weekdays, 20/– per round (15/– with member), 35/– per day (30/– with member)
Weekends, 40/– per round (15/– with member), 40/– per day (30/– with member)
Weekly tickets £7

18 holes, 6484 yards

	yards		yards
1st hole	429	10th hole	360
2nd hole	358	11th hole	372
3rd hole	222	12th hole	325
4th hole	436	13th hole	430
5th hole	436	14th hole	504
6th hole	155	15th hole	440
7th hole	469	16th hole	154
8th hole	175	17th hole	408
9th hole	382	18th hole	429

Established in 1887, Royal St. George's is one of our greatest golf clubs, steeped in tradition and history. The turf at Sandwich gives lies one dreams about, the ball is always 'lying a treat' so, with larks singing and the sun shining on the waters of Pegwell, it is a golfer's heaven:

The course, of the 'out-and-back' variety, is really in two unequal halves. It is some 400 yards shorter going out and, with three short holes in this half, one's score has to be made by the 8th hole.

Bernard Darwin, our Boswell of golf, said: "I think it is the beauty and the extraordinary solitude of Sandwich which endears it to the golfers. We wind about in dells and hollows among the great hills, alone in the midst of a multitude, and hardly ever realise that there are others playing on the links until we meet them at luncheon."

I have known Sandwich since I was a boy. I had my first big success there in 1934 when I won the Open Championship with a 283 total, which included a 65, a score still not beaten in the Open; Tony Jacklin did a 64 during the Masters' Tournament in 1967.

I well remember the final day of play in the 1938 Open at Sandwich, won by R. A. Whitcombe. I drove the 2nd green and the 11th green in one round, 358 yards and 384 yards, and I remember seeing Alfred Padgham chipping back to the green at the 11th, having overdriven the green.

I lost that Open by going out-of-bounds at the long 14th hole, 520 yards, with my second shot in the gale; this I would regard as the toughest hole on the course.

Bobby Locke and Harry Bradshaw had a great tussle there in the 1949 Open, when Bradshaw experienced the most amazing of all Championship mishaps. His first round of 69 led the field and he was doing well in the second until he drove his ball into the rough at the 5th and found it lodged in the bottom of a broken beer bottle. He played his ball from the inside of the bottle. Had he picked and dropped – no penalty – he could certainly have had a putt for a 4, and even a 5 meant a win. With a total of 283 he tied with Locke, but in the play-off Bradshaw was beaten by twelve strokes.

Albert E. Whiting, professional, writes:

Royal St. George's is an open seaside links, with sand dunes, coarse rough, undulating greens and deep sand bunkers. The course, 6728 yards in length, has been the scene of nine Open Championships and nine Amateur Championships, as well as Walker Cup matches.

My father followed Tom Varden – brother of the famous Harry – as professional here in 1911. I have been connected with the club for over fifty years now and have enjoyed every moment of it, working for a fine bunch of members.

I think the 5th is our toughest hole, that dogleg to the left played over 'The Sahara', a huge sandy area which occupies about a quarter of this 451 yards long hole. The 14th, being the longest hole and having an out-of-bounds fence all along the right hand side, worries some players.

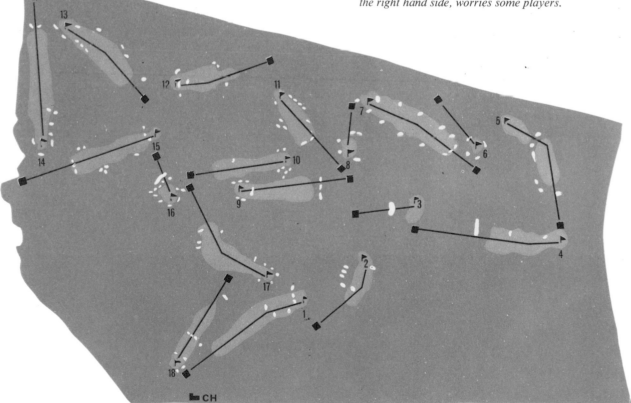

Royal Mid-Surrey Golf Club

Old Deer Park, Richmond, Surrey

Tel: Richmond 1677

Secretary: L. D. Warne
Tel: Richmond 1894

Nearest station: Richmond, 5 minutes

Hotel: Marshead Hotel, Richmond Hill

Course record: Professional, 65 by J. Adams

Visitors' fees: Weekdays 30/– per round (5/– with member)
30/– per day (10/– with member)
At weekends visitors must be accompanied by an introducing member

18 holes, 6435 yards

	yards		yards
1st hole	235	10th hole	465
2nd hole	525	11th hole	135
3rd hole	380	12th hole	460
4th hole	375	13th hole	330
5th hole	150	14th hole	490
6th hole	395	15th hole	485
7th hole	330	16th hole	210
8th hole	195	17th hole	440
9th hole	445	18th hole	390

These two courses of Royal Mid-Surrey lie on beautiful deer park turf next to London's famous Kew Gardens and bordered on another side by the river Thames. The club achieved Royal status in 1926 when the Prince of Wales became Club Captain.

The courses, planned in 1892, are flat, but cleverly designed and never easy to score on. The big men's course, 6435 yards, plays every yard of it. The ladies' course of 5530 yards is most entertaining. It lies within the bounds of the men's course and is part of the very strong and independent ladies' section. There is a small practice area and a magnificent well-spaced putting green.

I have always found the 10th hole of 465 yards the most difficult to get a par 4 at, the tee shot being narrow and the green hard to hit because of the steep front face to it which tends to throw the ball to the right and left.

J. H. Taylor – one of the famous old Triumvirate comprising Harry Vardon, J. H. Taylor and James Braid – was club professional at Royal Mid-Surrey for forty-seven years and made much golfing history during his stay with the club.

The present professional is James Adams, now one of our veteran players, who had the fullest swing in golf in his great days and a delicate putting touch.

One of the most revered members was S. H. Fry, eight times Amateur Billiard Champion and a scratch golfer who 'broke his age' innumerable times, even doing a 75 when over 80 years of age.

I was professional at Royal Mid-Surrey from 1946 to 1952 and I won my third Open Championship during this period. But my earliest souvenir of golfing at Mid-Surrey was in 1920 when my father took my brother Leslie and me to play with the great 'J.H.' on his own course to get his opinion on our golf. In presenting his comments later, in a letter to my father, J.H. noted that I had the better concentration. He often referred to this with satisfaction in later years when time had proved his judgement to have been correct.

James Adams, professional, writes:

Royal Mid-Surrey is a good test as a park course, being narrow and flat with many bunkers around the greens. The bunkers are quite short of the greens, however, which tests the player's judgement of distance, an essential quality of a good golfer. The holes appear straight but many of the greens are 'laid out' in such a way that you really can place your drive on a certain side of the fairway to make your second shot easier. This is a good golf feature and one which puts Royal Mid-Surrey under the heading of a 'thinker's course'. The greens are flattish in appearance but there are many almost unnoticeable borrows which I would describe as difficult.

I think the 3rd, a dogleg left, is the toughest hole. Trees stretch 150 yards on the left and with mounds on the right it needs a good drive on the right of the fairway to enable the player to see the green. A deceptive hollow twenty yards short of the green adds to the complications.

My best score is 62, made up of a run of six birdies – a once in a lifetime event.

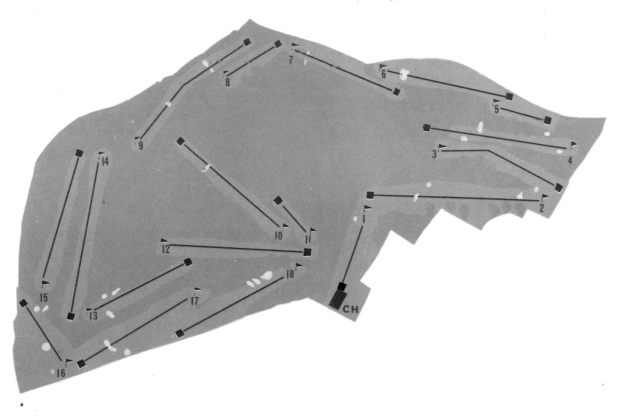

Manor House Hotel Golf Club

Manor House Hotel, Moretonhampstead, Devon

Tel: Moretonhampstead 355

Secretary: J. M. Whittingham

Nearest station: Exeter

Nearest hotel: Manor House Hotel

Course record: 66 by Norman Sutton, Exeter, West of England Championship 1959

Visitors' fees: Weekdays, 12/6 per day
Weekends, 20/– per day

18 holes, 6260 yards

1st hole	310	10th hole	175
2nd hole	400	11th hole	480
3rd hole	160	12th hole	205
4th hole	530	13th hole	325
5th hole	410	14th hole	305
6th hole	165	15th hole	410
7th hole	390	16th hole	345
8th hole	405	17th hole	390
9th hole	425	18th hole	430

This hotel and golf club were part of the assets which went with the railway companies when they were nationalised in 1951. But as it was then a losing proposition it had to be liquidated with other unprofitable ventures. The course, designed by J. F. 'Aber' Abercrombie of Addington, was the grounds of the W. H. Smith family country house, sold to the railways as a hotel.

Mr Frank G. Hole, General Manager of the new Transport Hotels Group, asked me to take a look at it about that time to see if I had any ideas for improvements. Among my suggestions was one that the 18th green should be brought closer to the clubhouse – the course then ended 250 yards from the hotel. The course, with the 18th green 50 yards from the hotel, soon achieved well-deserved popularity, and golfer's enjoy this most luxurious small country hotel even more after teeing off against the hotel wall and ending back again almost to where they teed off.

This splendid course is now so much appreciated that golfers have to book their accommodation in advance. Life in this hotel closely follows the pleasant pattern of country house living in former days, when staff and efficient and willing service were always available.

Trees, gentle slopes, bubbling trout streams, smooth expansive fairways, distant views of Dartmoor from 800 feet up on Manor Tor, and the vivid colours of shrubs and flowers make it a delightful experience to play on this 6260 yard course, with its 18 holes of intriguing and testing quality.

If you do not know this remote part of Devon you will be enchanted; if you are a golf lover you will appreciate it even more. My memories of the Manor House Hotel and Golf Course are of the luxurious country house atmosphere, with the fire blazing brightly in the lounge and superb service, and the beauty of those first nine holes.

Angus MacDonald, professional, writes:
This is a parkland type course on which the first nine holes are the most difficult, for alongside them meanders the trout-filled River Bovey, and even the gifted player is lucky to keep his ball above water level. The second nine holes are more open, and shorter in length. The greens are tricky, most of them having quite a bit of borrow on them. I regard the 7th hole as being one of the finest golfing holes in the country. The fairway, narrow in comparison with most of the others, has the river in the middle of it for 200 yards; then the river turns away to the right side of the fairway and runs up to the green, which makes the entrance to this green very narrow. This hole is usually played against the prevailing wind from the west, which makes it play much longer than 390 yards.

25

West Hill Golf Club

Brookwood, Surrey

Tel: Brookwood 2110

Secretary: Mrs. B. Crichton

Nearest station: Brookwood – ½ mile

Nearest hotels: The Wheatsheaf, Woking;
Mayford Manor, Woking;
Worplesdon Place, Worplesdon.

Course record: Professional, 67, by E. R. Whitcombe,
T. H. Cotton, A. Havers, A. J. Lacey
and J. Adams.

Visitors' fees: Weekdays 20/– per round
(10/– with member);
40/– per day (20/– with member);

Weekends 40/– per round
(20/– with member);
40/– per day (25/– with member).

18 holes, 6407 yards

	yards		yards
1st hole	402	10th hole	430
2nd hole	360	11th hole	396
3rd hole	458	12th hole	304
4th hole	190	13th hole	157
5th hole	510	14th hole	466
6th hole	433	15th hole	220
7th hole	175	16th hole	390
8th hole	388	17th hole	510
9th hole	176	18th hole	442

West Hill is another course I like to show to American visitors, for this beautiful golf course with its wealth of trees and heather is surely one of Surrey's beauty spots. It is also a delightful course to play on in any weather, the variety of the holes providing a first class test for any golfer.

This course is unique in having been founded in 1910 by a lady golfer, Mrs. Geoffrey Lubbock, at a time when ladies were not admitted to membership in any local golf club. Mrs. Lubbock decided to form a club of her own and that was the start of West Hill.

The course was superbly laid out by C. Butchart, a Scottish professional who became club professional. Very few alterations have been made to the original course, which is considered a showpiece of golfing planning. Perhaps the fact that it has five short holes – when St. Andrews has only two and Carnoustie five – makes low scoring feats easier, but the 15th at West Hill is definitely in the running for the best short hole in Britain.

I once had a shared course record of 67 there with E. R. Whitcombe, Arthur Havers, A. J. Lacey and Jimmy Adams – all heroes of the past – while a local amateur and Club Captain, W. A. Murray, has a 66 to his credit.

This is again an 'out and back' course, a handicap for the golfing crowds of today, but a handicap shared by many of the popular clubs.

In this particular corner of Surrey there are a number of superb courses but West Hill is in no way inferior to any of them. I think it is a great course.

George Evans, professional, writes:

Set among heather and pine trees West Hill is a testing course, not too hilly but with enough undulations to make it interesting. The greens are very good but difficult to read. Features of the course are the little stream which crosses many holes and the cross strips of heather on the fairways.

The 220-yard 15th hole is probably the best short hole in the country, indeed this hole has been copied in America. The wind is nearly always against the player at this hole and there are fifteen bunkers on the way, as well as those all round the plateau green. The 6th is also a very fine hole. The drive is up a slight slope and below is the green, bordered on the right by heather and trees and with a big bunker on the left. A very accurate second shot is needed here.

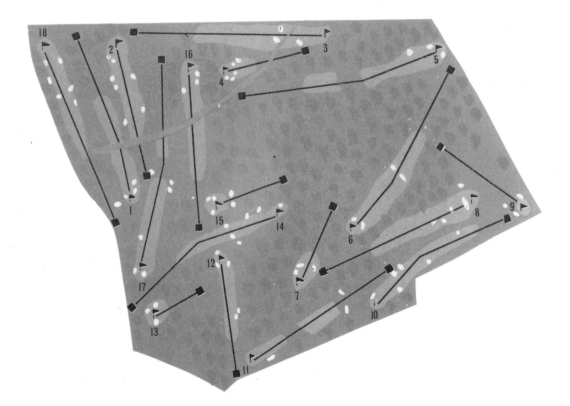

Sunningdale Golf Club

Sunningdale, Berks

Tel: Ascot 21681, 20128

Secretary: Colonel R. E. S. Yeldham, C.B.E.

Nearest station: Sunningdale — $\frac{1}{4}$ mile

Course record:
Old Course: 63 by N. G. von Nida
New Course: 64 by G. J. Player

Visitors' fees: Weekdays 50/− (20/− with member).
Weekends limited to members and
guests playing with members.

Length of Courses:
Old Course: 18 holes, 6348 yards
New Course: 18 holes, 6521 yards

	Old Course yards	New Course yards		Old Course yards	New Course yards
1st hole	492	459	10th hole	462	212
2nd hole	454	180	11th hole	299	448
3rd hole	296	394	12th hole	422	389
4th hole	165	440	13th hole	178	550
5th hole	394	177	14th hole	476	185
6th hole	392	436	15th hole	229	406
7th hole	390	371	16th hole	418	381
8th hole	168	400	17th hole	421	178
9th hole	272	439	18th hole	420	476

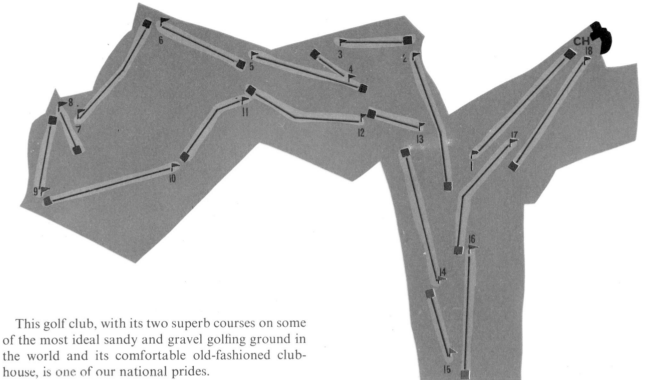

This golf club, with its two superb courses on some of the most ideal sandy and gravel golfing ground in the world and its comfortable old-fashioned club-house, is one of our national prides.

The Old Course, one of the world's famous courses, was designed by Willie Park and built in 1900. It is a most pleasant course to play, even from the back tees, now about 6500 yards. An honest but not too severe test of golf, it gives a square deal to players of every conceivable standard of hitting power and of every handicap. The New Course, designed by W. H. Colt in 1922, is slightly larger and is more difficult for the club golfer. Just across the road from the club-house is the Ladies' Course, 18 holes of very interesting golf on the same ground as the two big courses but run independently.

It is true to say that the Old Course, an out and back layout, is one of the most beautiful inland golf courses in the game. I have always found the 15th hole on this course to be one of the most difficult par 3s in golf. The bunker on the left of the green, in the words of Bernard Darwin, "sucks in balls like a whirlpool", and from the shelter of some trees it is difficult to judge the wind across the open heathland which surrounds this green. The tee shot from the 10th tee – an elevated one on to a well bunkered fairway below – is one of the most inspiring in the game.

Very many major golfing events are staged at Sunningdale because it has 36 holes to offer as well as other facilities, such as a practice area and fairly adequate parking space.

The job of professional at Sunningdale is considered one of the plums of the profession. The first professional there was Jack White, who won the 1904 Open Championship at Sandwich. After Jack came Ernest Sales, Michael Bingham, Percy Broomer, and now Arthur Lees carries on the tradition of running one of the best golf shops in the country.

As everyone wants to claim that he has 'played' Sunningdale, green fees are not cheap, but golfing on these courses is a pleasure not to be missed.

Arthur Lees, professional, writes:
Sunningdale is a parkland course, surrounded by pine and birch trees, with heather, gorse and wild flowers growing profusely along the fairways.

Although individual rounds of 65, 64 and 63 have been made on the Old Course – the latter score being the present record held by Norman von Nida – probably the two most famous rounds were those of 66 and 68 played by Bobby Jones in the qualifying round of the 1926 Open Championship, mainly because the two rounds contained only one 5 and one 2.

Royal Liverpool Golf Club

Meols Drive, Hoylake, Cheshire

Tel: Hoylake 1450
Secretary: H. G. MacPherson
Tel: Hoylake 4676
Nearest station: Hoylake — 5 minutes
Hotel: Stanley Hotel, Hoylake
Course record: Professional,
        67 by Gary Player and
        Roberto de Vicenzo
Visitors' fees: Weekdays and Weekends
        40/— per round or day

18 holes, 6740 yards

	yards		yards
1st hole	421	10th hole	404
2nd hole	365	11th hole	201
3rd hole	491	12th hole	395
4th hole	179	13th hole	158
5th hole	445	14th hole	501
6th hole	364	15th hole	459
7th hole	193	16th hole	504
8th hole	476	17th hole	391
9th hole	393	18th hole	400

Royal Liverpool, celebrating its centenary in 1969, is one of our great seaside links and has long been recognised as a great test of golf.

The course has been regularly altered since I first played on it in 1930. Sometimes I am out of sympathy with these alterations, as very soon no course will be left for posterity to see as it was when golfers first knew it, therefore no comparison will be possible in the standards of play. While courses are lengthened continually they are softened up with watering, making them easier and slower to pitch and putt on. Gone for ever are the very slick greens we all dreaded at Hoylake, so true and so dangerous.

Royal Liverpool is by no means photogenic; it is on flat land with some low sandhills. The winds make this course, but this out-and-back layout in out-of-bound boundaries is a test of nerve and skill at any time, though perhaps 25% less nerve-racking now that the greens hold so well.

The last five holes are considered one of golf's toughest finishes and if your score is not made by the 13th hole you have a hard time holding on to level fours in the run-in.

Professional Campbell Adamson thinks the 17th hole is the killer. When Fred Daly won the Open in 1947 the gods were on his side: his second shot to the 17th hole struck a strand of wire and bounced back into play. At the same 17th hole Alfred Padgham, who won the 1936 Open, played his second shot safe and short of the narrow dangerous green with the fence right on the edge of the putting surface, and holed out with his putter from miles away for a 3 – the hole was out of sight!

Three legendary names from this English home of golf are those of John Ball, Harold Hilton and Jack Graham.

A final tribute to Royal Liverpool from Bernard Darwin, whose able pen I have always admired. "Although the links of Hoylake belong primarily to the Royal Liverpool Golf Club," he wrote, "they belong to the world for the great part they have played in the history of the game."

Campbell Adamson, professional, writes:

This is a long testing links, probably one of the toughest in Britain. Situated at the tip of the Wirral Peninsula, it stands at the junction of the rivers Dee and Mersey where they run into the Irish Sea. It is, therefore, open to its main hazard – strong winds – at all times.

This club has always been very closely linked with amateur golf. It was here that the tournament now acknowledged as the first Amateur Championship was held, Here, too, was held the first international match between England and Scotland, the first match between Britain and the United States and the first English Amateur Championship. The club has been host to the Open Championship on ten occasions, and the News of the World *Matchplay, Dunlop Masters and other professional tournaments have also been staged here.*

To name the toughest hole at Royal Liverpool is a problem – I find no easy holes here. The most difficult are probably the 17th, when the west wind blows strongly towards the road, and the 1st hole when it becomes the 19th and sudden death in matchplay, with the out-of-bounds practice area a real menace.

The practice area of 275 by 200 yards is ample during the week, but in the summer evenings and at weekends it is hardly big enough. On medal days I run it as a driving range, hiring out balls to competitors for a warm-up session, with no collection worries, before play.

Royal Cinque Ports Golf Club

Golf Road, Deal, Kent

Tel: Deal 328

Secretary: T. C. M. Dickinson
Tel: Deal 7

Nearest station: Deal, 1½ miles

Hotels: Royal Hotel, Deal;
Bell Hotel, Sandwich

Course record: Amateur, 65 by M. F. Bonallack
Professional, 67 by P. Allis and
J. Adams

Visitors' fees: £2 per round, Saturdays, Sundays and
Bank Holidays
£2 10s. per day Saturdays, Sundays
and Bank Holidays
20/– per round weekdays
30/– per day weekdays

18 holes, 6384 yards

	yards		yards
1st hole	328	10th hole	368
2nd hole	366	11th hole	388
3rd hole	449	12th hole	426
4th hole	153	13th hole	412
5th hole	487	14th hole	199
6th hole	293	15th hole	414
7th hole	341	16th hole	456
8th hole	154	17th hole	364
9th hole	390	18th hole	396

This famous links, right on the shore of the English Channel and defended from the high tides by a shingle bank, was designed in 1892 and took its royal title in 1908 when the then Prince of Wales became its president.

The course is 6659 yards, and is recognised as a superb test of skill. Michael Bonallack, our crack amateur, holed the course in 65 strokes in 1964 – a great round!

It is an 'out and back' course, running north and south from the outskirts of the pretty little town of Deal, along the coast to the beginning of Sandwich Bay. The wind is usually southwest, so a golfer must 'make' his round in the first eleven holes, all in the same direction except for the first, and then fight back against the wind. Many golfers dislike Deal because of the endless humps and hollows of the fairways, which can give desperate stances and bring more than average luck into the game.

There have been times here when the sea has breached the shingle wall and salt water has ruined some fairways; but this has not happened for some time and all is well now, for the greens and fairways are true and of real seaside texture.

The Open Championship was last played here in 1920, when George Duncan scored his only win in this old event. It is not, unfortunately, an ideal course for crowds, but the facilities and the location of the clubhouse, close to the town, make it a delightful holiday course. Every spring the Holford Hewitt Public Schools Tournament by team foursomes is held here, and hundreds of golfers turn up to enjoy the gathering and the golf.

This is a tough course to score on, but easy to walk; it is one of the courses where it pays to know what shot is *on* from a particular stance or lie, where one must use one's judgment and treat golf as a percentage game. Long drives can be made when the ball hits a fortunate down slope on the pitch, or the same sort of drive can be pitifully short from striking a steep up-slope. But this is golfing at Deal: you either like this type of golf or you do not. Stroke 1 on the card is the 13th hole, 426 yards from the Championship Tee.

ROYAL CINQUE PORTS——
Reg Moore, professional, writes:

This famous old club began in 1892, our 75th anniversary was held in 1967.

Royal Cinque Ports is a typical links course, with quite wide fairways undulating through the dunes and fairly large relatively flat greens, which are some of the finest in the country. The course can and does provide a test for the mighty, but it also provides excellent golf for the more modest player. The practice area is 130 yards wide by 300 yards long and we have a practice putting green and bunker.

All the principal Championships have been played here. Past captains of the club include Bernard Darwin and Halford Hewitt, and Lionel Munn and Douglas Grant are past members.

Over the years many famous golfers have written in praise of this course. Among the tributes on display at the clubhouse are those penned by Harry Vardon, James Braid, Ted Ray, George Duncan, Ben Sayers, Francis Ouimet, Arnaud Massey, J. H. Taylor, Cyril Tolley and Chick Evans.

The 16th hole is, in my opinion, the most difficult. Some 474 yards in length, it is a par 4, with a carry of about 170 yards from the tee over some bunkers to a quite wide fairway, which slopes away slightly on both sides. The green is sited on a plateau, which again falls away on both sides, with quite rugged country on the right of the green. This shot is played into the prevailing wind and must be one of the longest 4s in golf.

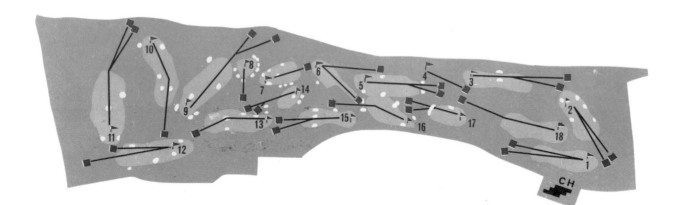

Worplesdon Golf Club

Woking, Surrey

Tel: Brookwood 2277

Secretary: Major W. Hughes, M.B.E.

Off main trunk road from Bagshot to Guildford — A322

Nearest hotel: Wheatsheaf Hotel, Woking

Course record: Amateur, 64 by D. W. Frame

Visitors' fees: Weekdays, 30/— per day, 20/— per round.
Weekends and Bank Holidays, 40/— per round or day.
Weekend visitors must be introduced.

18 holes, 6304 yards

	yards		yards
1st hole	365	10th hole	138
2nd hole	394	11th hole	520
3rd hole	385	12th hole	475
4th hole	168	13th hole	175
5th hole	412	14th hole	388
6th hole	476	15th hole	500
7th hole	183	16th hole	164
8th hole	387	17th hole	400
9th hole	336	18th hole	438

Cut out of a wilderness of trees, gorse and heather, Worplesdon is one of the prettiest and most popular courses in this nature-built golfing area of Surrey. The holes wander about in the woodland, so that the enjoyment of the game is enhanced by a marvellous sense of peace and pleasant solitude.

The course, 6304 yards long, was designed by J. F. Abercromby in 1908 and has been little altered. It is again an 'out-and-back' plan.

The 10th hole, just 138 yards across a 60-yard wide pond, is one of the most picturesque holes I know. Silver birch, chestnut, oak trees and rhododendrons make a spectacular background for this deceiving hole. I like the touching story about the old lady golfer who could not carry her ball across the pond at this hole, so she used to putt it all around the pond on the path.

Worplesdon is the home of the famous Open Mixed Amateur Foursomes, played in October. This event, run with the friendly charm of a country houseparty, is one of the British golfing institutions and has always an overfull entry list. If you want to turn the golfing clock back, then go to see the Foursomes and rejoice that a successful tournament can be run without massive scoreboards and hordes of attendants. Incidentally, the honour board for this event reads like a golfing Who's Who.

Two famous golfing names always associated with Worplesdon are those of Roger and Joyce Wethered, now Lady Heathcote Amory, the Club's President. This brother and sister team won all the top golfing honours in the twenties and thirties.

Whenever I have played at Worplesdon – which has been, I regret, all too seldom – I have always fervently hoped that this course would be left exactly as it is so that golfers of the future might see what a members' course of our generation looked like, for Worplesdon seems to have everything for every standard of play.

Alan Waters, professional, writes:

Worplesdon is one of the heather and pine type courses found throughout Surrey, not a long course by some standards, but one which demands accuracy. Our greens have only slight borrows and are very true and not too tricky.

I would consider the 5th and 9th our most testing holes. The 5th, 412 yards, is an admirable two-shotter; the drive must first be placed between heather on the right and a magnetic bunker on the left. For the second shot the green, a rather long and narrow one, is well guarded by nature with a formation of grassy ridges and hollows. There are also two bunkers set to gather the wayward stroke. The 9th hole, 336 yards, has a rather alarming tee-shot in which players must skirt a tall wood and ditch on the right and take care not to hook out-of-bounds on the left.

Little Aston Golf Club

Tel: Streetly 2066

Hon. Secretary: N. H. Russell

Nearest station: Streetly — $1\frac{1}{4}$ miles

Hotel: Penns Hall Hotel, Walmley

Visitors' fees: Weekdays 35/— per day
(5/— with member);

Weekends and Bank Holidays
45/— per day (10/— with member).

18 holes, 6693 yards

	yards		yards
1st hole	392	10th hole	463
2nd hole	443	11th hole	382
3rd hole	500	12th hole	482
4th hole	329	13th hole	156
5th hole	159	14th hole	323
6th hole	427	15th hole	548
7th hole	368	16th hole	413
8th hole	392	17th hole	361
9th hole	179	18th hole	386

This is a fine parkland course with a subsoil of sand and gravel, situated in a beautiful woodland setting only nine miles from the centre of Birmingham. Harry Vardon planned the first layout – an out-and-back one as it is today – but minor alterations were later made by W. H. Colt and former club professional M. J. Lewis.

A beautiful course in acres of heather, it has been called the Sunningdale of the Midlands. The turf is excellent, the fairway lies are superb and the large greens are true and keen and well-protected. A lake adjoins the 17th green.

There are many great holes at Little Aston, so that I find it difficult to name the toughest one. But the innocent-looking 15th hole, of 548 yards, is a hard par 5. A mound crosses the fairway halfway up the hole and there are cross bunkers to be carried for the second shot with a brassie. Club members find the slightly uphill 2nd hole, with a closely guarded green, a handful.

This is a course fit for heroes to play over, with everything to test a golfer.

Charles H. Ward, professional, writes:

Little Aston came into being in 1908. This makes it a veteran among golf clubs in the Midlands, although sixty-one years is a mere fraction in the history of a game whose beginnings are lost in antiquity.

The surroundings here are very pleasant; the length of the course is as near an ideal as possible to cater for golfers of varying degrees of proficiency; the holes are sporting and demand all kinds of play, and the greens, with water laid on to each, are fairly fast.

I think the 10th hole, a long dogleg to the left, is the finest hole on the course for every type of player. The trees on the left are inclined to attract the drive, but only the long hitter dare attempt the long carry. The handicap player can drive well up the right with safety and then use a wood again, playing short of a cross bunker and leaving a firm No. 7 or 8 iron to the open green. The long hitter, having made the carry, is well within reach of the green with a spoon; a risky tee-shot can save a stroke from par, or ruin a card.

Little Aston has been host to many professional tournaments and the English Amateur Championship has been played here twice, in 1927 and 1948.

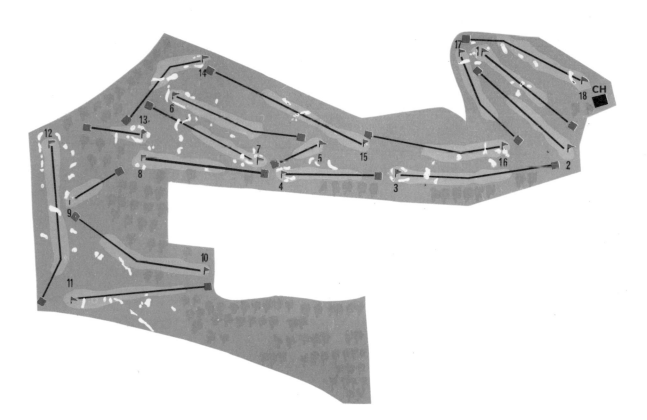

Royal Wimbledon Golf Club

29 Camp Road, Wimbledon Common, London SW19

Tel: Wimbledon 0055
Secretary: E. Scudamore
Nearest station: Wimbledon – 1 mile
Course record: Professional, 71 by R. Burton
Visitors' fees: on introduction by a member:
25/– per round, 35/– per day.

18 holes, 6355 yards

	yards		yards
1st hole	420	10th hole	480
2nd hole	440	11th hole	415
3rd hole	375	12th hole	450
4th hole	405	13th hole	165
5th hole	170	14th hole	450
6th hole	265	15th hole	435
7th hole	485	16th hole	390
8th hole	225	17th hole	150
9th hole	280	18th hole	355

This course, remodelled by H. S. Colt, provides a long and difficult test of golf and, especially when the ground is slow in winter, it will amply reward the strong hitter. The greens are all excellent and much faster than most inland greens so that putting never degenerates into mere slogging.

One of the best holes on the course is the 12th – a 450 yard par 4, a semi dogleg to the right, with both sides of the fairway lined with gorse and heather. The second shot, from a good drive to a plateau green trapped at the righthand corner, is particularly difficult.

There are two starting points on this course and there is a small practice area. Outside the clubhouse is a large 18-hole putting green, which is considered the best in the country. Each year the club stages a putting tournament over five evenings, taking the teams from various club, societies and members of Old Boys' Golfing Societies.

Among the curious golfing freaks which have occurred at Royal Wimbledon was the holing in one at the 6th hole, 265 yards, by His Royal Highness the Duke of Windsor, when he was Prince of Wales and Captain of Royal Wimbledon.

Russell Dailey, professional, writes:

Royal Wimbledon Golf Club was established by the London Scottish Rifle Volunteer Corps, under the presidency of Lord Elcho, in 1865. It is an 18-hole course on high ground bordering Wimbledon Common.

The course is heavily wooded, with narrow undulating fairways where accuracy from the tee is most important and four holes lie in a valley. The greens have subtle slopes where it pays to have local knowledge.

The 4th hole – a par 4 of 405 yards – is probably the toughest hole for the handicap golfer who, after a good shot, is left with a 200 yard second shot to a small elevated green bordered by trees and gorse bushes.

The Professional record stands at 71 by Dick Burton and the Amateur record is 67 by Dr. F. A. Simmonds. I have the privilege of holding the lowest score of 63.

Some well-known members of Royal Wimbledon include Lord Rothschild, Lord Wilberforce, Roger Wethered, Arnold Bentley and Kenneth More.

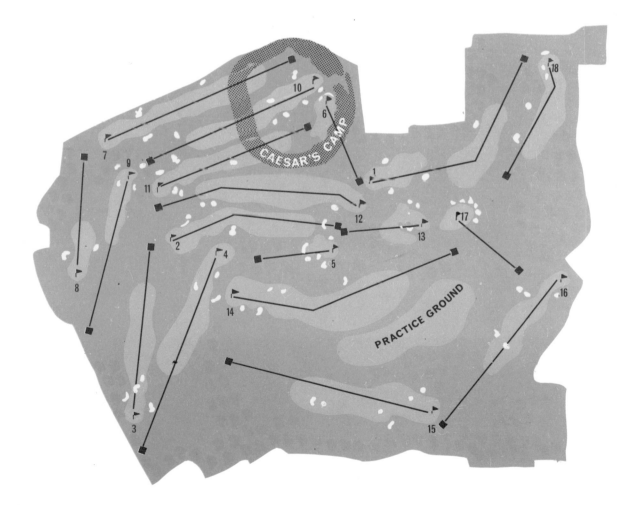

Crowborough Beacon Golf Club

Crowborough, Sussex

Tel: Crowborough 61511
Secretary: W. Lundie-Rees
Nearest station: Jarvis Brook — 2 miles
Hotel: Crest Hotel, Crowborough
Course record: 66 by C. Macey, Professional, and L. Wickens, Amateur
Visitors' fees: Weekdays 15/– per round, 20/– per day; Saturdays 31/6 per round.

18 holes, 6245 yards

	yards		yards
1st hole	411	10th hole	467
2nd hole	450	11th hole	324
3rd hole	146	12th hole	416
4th hole	363	13th hole	132
5th hole	363	14th hole	483
6th hole	196	15th hole	367
7th hole	498	16th hole	340
8th hole	321	17th hole	139
9th hole	391	18th hole	438

Founded in 1895, Crowborough Beacon is one of the oldest golf courses in the south. It occupies some three hundred acres of the Manor of Allchorns, 780 feet above sea level, and is a testing heathland course with natural hazards.

This course grew from an original layout of 9 holes to 14 holes and then to a full 18 in 1897. Since then it has been the scene of many county events and a few exhibition and challenge matches. A match between James Braid and American champion Horace Rawlin was played here on 5th March 1897 and resulted in a win for Braid with the record score of 81.

Among Crowborough's famous members were Sir Arthur Conan Doyle; the Hon. Michael Scott, who still holds the record as being the oldest player to win the Amateur Championship at fifty-five years, and that wide-stanced amateur Colonel C. O. Hezlett.

David White, professional, writes:

The greens at Crowborough Beacon are always in excellent condition. They are fairly tricky, although they are never cut short as there is no water laid on and they are, therefore, fairly slow.

No record is available of the architect of the original course in 1895, but the first committee consisted of F. H. Gresson, P. H. Phillips, Colonel Holland, Major Spens, H. C. Malden and H. J. Verrall.

The most recent change to the course was made for the purpose of cutting out some of the drag, for the hilly course could be a bit hard on some of the older members. The toughest hole is, in my opinion, the 450-yard 2nd. A downhill righthand dogleg sloping to the right calls for a long and accurate drive to give any chance for a short to the green, which is guarded by a fifteen-foot gulley cutting into the fairway. The unwatered green will not hold, so you are compelled to run the shot in from the left. In the clubhouse is mounted a golf ball which Major Blair holed with his second shot at this hole.

The average player considers the 7th to be the most difficult hole. Here the fairway slopes to the left into rough and gorse, and the second shot – which players usually find difficult – is blind over a road, with the green guarded by heather on the right.

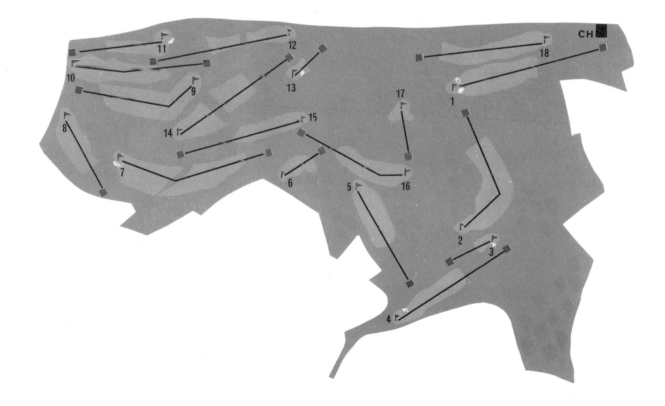

41

Lindrick Golf Club

Lindrick Common, near Worksop, Notts

Tel: Shireoaks 219

Secretary: Eric Taylor

Nearest station: Worksop – 3 miles

Nearest hotels: Royal Hotel, Worksop;
Old Bell Hotel, Barnby Moor

Course record: Professional, 66 by H. Weetman and
P. W. Thomson

Visitors' fees: Weekdays, 20/– per round, 30/– per
day. Weekends and Bank Holidays,
40/– per round, 50/– per day

18 holes, 6555 yards

	yards		yards
1st hole	400	10th hole	372
2nd hole	358	11th hole	170
3rd hole	164	12th hole	460
4th hole	472	13th hole	470
5th hole	430	14th hole	516
6th hole	138	15th hole	351
7th hole	427	16th hole	486
8th hole	318	17th hole	387
9th hole	436	18th hole	200

The Lindrick Golf Club was formed in 1891. It was originally called the Sheffield and District Golf Club, but forty years later it took its name from the common on which it is situated. The common was a natural site for a golf course: a river, a quarry or two, endless stretches of golden gorse. Limestone rock is very near the surface and bunkers have to be blasted out.

This dry heathland course is one of the best inland courses in the country because of its interesting layout and the wonderful quality of fairways and greens.

The 5th green is located at the spot where Yorkshire, Derbyshire and Nottinghamshire join, and cock fights were held on this green years ago.

This 'out-and-back' course is steeped in country and international golfing history. Braid, Taylor and Williamson played here in an exhibition match organised by the club in 1905. Braid's terms were 6 guineas plus expenses; Taylor's, £7.10.0 plus expenses and Williamson's 3 guineas, including expenses. Another such match in 1919 in which Abe Mitchell, Ray, Tom Williamson and R. Jacobs – father of present professional John Jacobs – took part, cost £58 to put on. What would our television golfing stars of today say to such pay, even allowing for devaluation?

There is a natural charm about Lindrick. At first it looks like many of our common land courses. But it is completely different, and worth any detour to play it.

John A. Jacobs, professional, writes:

When I came to Lindrick in 1924, as assistant professional, the course was open common land, but since then oaks and silver birches have been planted. In those days the 2nd and 18th holes required second shots over the main A57 road. As road traffic mounted this became a hazard for both golfer and motorist and, in 1926, the 2nd hole was made into a dogleg left and the 18th became a short hole, cutting out the short 16th. These have been the only alterations since the course was originally designed.

The 472 yards 4th hole causes the most trouble as you are playing a blind second into the green. Bernard Darwin, our great golf scribe, said this hole was the worst on the course, but he added that it must never, on any account, be altered.

The course ends with a short hole, a long well-bunkered one-shotter of 200 yards, with its green lying just below the clubhouse terrace, making a real grandstand finish.

Peter Thomson and Harry Weetman hold the professional record for the course with 66, but an amateur, Dr. D. F. Livingston, playing off a 4 handicap, returned a gross 65.

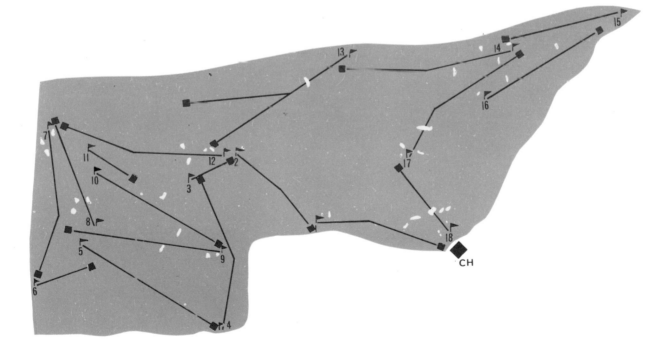

Thorpe Hall Golf Club

Thorpe Bay, Essex

Tel: Southend 78575
Secretary: Major Roy G. Emmett
Nearest station: Thorpe Bay – 5 minutes
Hotels: Westcliff Hotel;
      Overcliff Hotel, Westcliff-on-Sea.
Visitors' fees: Weekdays 20/– per day;

      Saturdays and Bank holidays
      30/– per day;

      Sundays (afternoons only)
      40/– per round (10/– with member).

18 holes, 6260 yards

	yards		yards
1st hole	361	10th hole	283
2nd hole	368	11th hole	503
3rd hole	167	12th hole	382
4th hole	500	13th hole	128
5th hole	175	14th hole	525
6th hole	463	15th hole	371
7th hole	189	16th hole	180
8th hole	585	17th hole	421
9th hole	318	18th hole	341

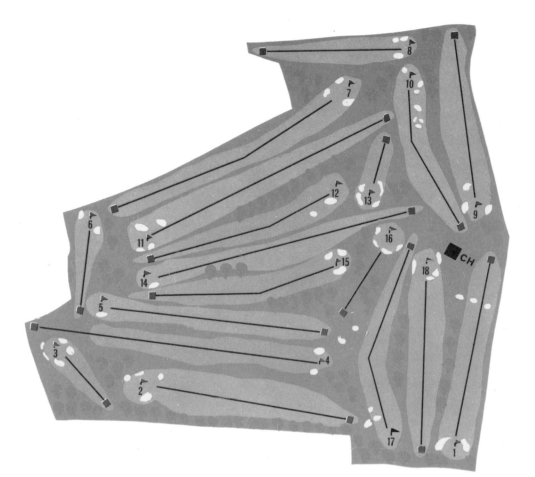

Thorpe Hall, the nearest seaside course to London, has the unusual distinction of being a first class parkland course by the sea. It is playable all the year round.

Golf can be a pleasure here for without any climbs there is still an infinite variety in the holes. It is a testing course and good figures are not easy. Water ditches are among the chief hazards and there is always a wind to add to the subtleties and natural hazards, so that the course plays longer than the actual yardage.

Geoffrey Gledhill, professional, writes:

Thorpe Hall Golf Club, opened in 1906, is a lovely parkland course, situated within 200 yards of the sea front in the residential area of Thorpe Bay. The greens are of good texture, but with tricky undulations and difficult to read.

Two new holes have recently been added to this very testing course. The 5th, a par 3 of 175 yards, requires a very accurate tee shot, with considerable flight to the elevated and heavily bunkered green. The 8th, a 585-yard par 5 hole, is probably one of the longest holes in the country and requires two long and well placed wooden club shots to ensure a good position from which to play to the small and heavily guarded green. I consider this hole to be the most difficult for the average club member.

The most testing hole for myself and for all low-handicap players is the 17th, a par 4 of 421 yards. This is a dogleg hole needing a long straight drive and long iron or wood to a difficult sloping green. Each stroke must be hit with precision and this is a most satisfying hole at which to make a par.

There is no official course record since this new layout was created but I have had a round of 66 and Michael Bonallack has done 65. The membership includes the famous golfing family of Bonallack.

Addington Golf Club

Shirley Church Road, Addington, Surrey

Tel: Spring Park 1055

Nearest station: East Croydon, 2½ miles

Hotels: Elgin Court Hotel, Croydon;
Selsdon Park Hotel, Sanderstead

Visitors' fees: Weekdays 25/– per day
Weekends 40/– per day

18 holes, 6216 yards

	yards		yards
1st hole	166	10th hole	356
2nd hole	555	11th hole	135
3rd hole	215	12th hole	470
4th hole	435	13th hole	230
5th hole	440	14th hole	365
6th hole	390	15th hole	441
7th hole	150	16th hole	494
8th hole	410	17th hole	180
9th hole	355	18th hole	429

Addington is a superb course, built by J. F. Abercromby in 1914, and featuring all manner of natural pitfalls, which are so typical of Abercromby golf architecture.

One of the practical advantages of the course is its proximity to London: ten miles, or just thirty minutes by car from the West End, given luck with the traffic lights but never exceeding the speed limits.

On arrival you will enter a golfing paradise of heather, pine, silver birch and bracken, with not a house in sight: a stretch of nature's own golf course land. It has remained unchanged and unspoilt since it was laid out in 1914 but, like so many courses of that era and earlier, it has only one starting point. I think the trestle bridges over deep, heathlined dells are most attractive; they should be a feature of more of our courses instead of being such a rarity in our islands.

The course is 6316 yards, with no room to lengthen it but no need to do so. It is a pity it begins with a tough shot hole but, a most important advantage, it is dry as a bone, even in a wet English winter. There is a secluded practice area, 400 yards by 70 yards, with a sand bunker.

My first visit to Addington was with my father and a club member when I was about thirteen years old; my handicap then was probably around 10. I enjoyed my first round immensely, as I have done every succeeding one. Willie Ritchie was club professional then, and the two courses – the Old and the New – were just as good as any one 36 holes of golf in the world. Only the Old course now remains; the New was taken by the local Corporation for a housing estate.

Another personal memory of Addington is of many delicious lunches there between the two world wars, with Fried Sole the speciality, followed by Treacle Tart with the filling nearly an inch thick.

Like the club members mentioned by Bill Mitchell, I have always found the 5th a hard hole to judge. I never seemed to estimate the length of the shot I had to play. I suppose I should have paced it out and logged it, as do the champs of today.

Among the prominent amateur members of Addington, past and present, I would list John de Forest, Amateur Champion in 1932; Dr. J. A. Flaherty and his son, Peter; Kenneth Thom and Peter Banka; the Hartley brothers, Mike and Ken, and Robert and Charles Sweeny. The course record of 65 is held by K. G. Thom.

Bill Mitchell, professional, writes:

A heathland course, Addington offers the golfer every type of golf shot. The dogleg and semi-dogleg holes are a feature of the course, as are the hanging lies for the second shots, where skilful putting is required on the tricky sloping greens. At the 9th, 10th, 13th and 17th holes, the tee shots are played over ravines, trestle bridges rewarding the accurate golfer.

The toughest hole, in my opinion, is the 8th, a par 4 of 410 yards. You have to hit a drive of 230 yards to end exactly by a huge grassy mound right on the dogleg, and then play a 180 yards long shot to a green along a saddle-back fairway to a green which runs away from you. On the left and right of the green is real trouble, as the ground falls away on both sides steeply. Without a bunker this hole is quite a test.

Club members, however, find the 5th the most difficult hole. This hole measures 440 yards and is a par 4, semi-dogleg to the left. As the fairway slopes from right to left, it requires an accurate tee-shot. The uphill shot to the green is always played from a hanging lie. Three bunkers guard the green – two on the right and one 40 yards short which must be carried with the second shot.

Denham Golf Club

Tilehouse Lane, Denham, Bucks

Tel: Denham 2022
Secretary: E. Radbone, O.B.E.
Nearest station: Denham, ½ mile
Hotel: The Bull, Gerrards Cross
Course record: 68 by J. Sheridan
Visitors' fees: Weekdays 25/– per round
              (7/6 with member)
          40/– per day
              (7/6 with member)
       Weekends 12/6 with member
       Weekly tickets (Monday-Friday) 4 gns

18 holes, 6351 yards

	yards		yards
1st hole	358	10th hole	400
2nd hole	358	11th hole	346
3rd hole	404	12th hole	142
4th hole	426	13th hole	513
5th hole	205	14th hole	452
6th hole	382	15th hole	402
7th hole	427	16th hole	140
8th hole	183	17th hole	356
9th hole	459	18th hole	398

A golf course whose praises are strangely unsung, Denham is one of the best inland courses in the country. It enjoys a fine, high situation and a setting that is mainly open but partly wooded and secluded, on fine heathland and parkland: grand terrain for golf. The clubhouse, converted from some lovely old farm buildings, is delightful and blends perfectly into the scene.

The course, which is 6373 yards in length, was an original Colt design. It has remained more or less as it was first constructed, with one or two alterations carried out on the advice of James Braid and, more recently, by C. K. Cotton. The club itself was founded in 1912 and run by Major R. Way, the owner, as a proprietary club until it passed into the hands of the members in 1944.

The greens are renowned, looked after by Head Greenkeeper Alec Miller, a County player and Artisan Champion of 1967. The club is rightly proud of his golfing talent and his dedication to his job. Some years ago the Denham committee became the second club in the country to have automatic watering installed on the greens.

The standard of golf at Denham is high and the club can field a very strong young side, a dozen players with a 2 handicap or better.

John Sheridan, professional, writes:

Denham golf course commands the advantages of a country setting yet within easy reach of London by road and rail: half an hour in a car from Marble Arch, or an equally comfortable journey by rail from Marylebone to the club's own station.

The course supplies the good player with a fairly stern challenge while it is, at the same time, not too forbidding for the higher handicaps. This combination has made it very popular with societies.

I think the 6th and the 15th holes, 382 and 402 yards respectively, and both par 4s, are our best holes, because both of them demand nominated tee shots. My best score over the course has been a 62.

We rarely have any tournaments outside county and alliance level, but Denham is a course with character and beauty, of which the members are justly proud, and one which is always enjoyed by those who play it.

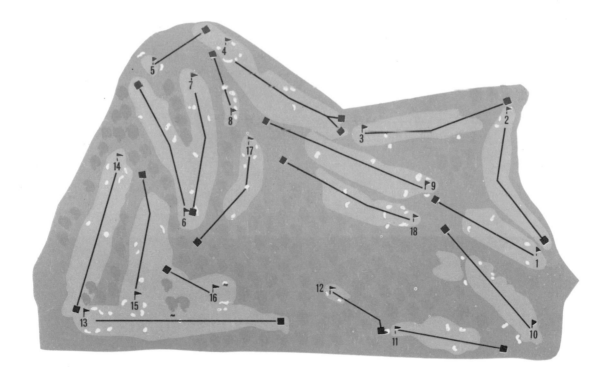

Royal Birkdale Golf Club
Waterloo Road, Birkdale, Southport, Lancs.

Tel: Southport 66020 and 66039

Secretary: Squadron Leader L. H. Clint
Tel: Southport 67920

Nearest stations: Hillside, ½ mile; Southport, 1½ miles

Hotels: Prince of Wales Hotel, Southport, and others

Course record: Professional, 68 by Tony Lema

Visitors' fees: £2 per round, 20/— after 4 p.m. (10/— with member.
Weekly tickets £8; fortnightly tickets £12

18 holes, 6678 yards

	yards		yards
1st hole	450	10th hole	376
2nd hole	427	11th hole	368
3rd hole	416	12th hole	180
4th hole	212	13th hole	437
5th hole	320	14th hole	202
6th hole	456	15th hole	530
7th hole	158	16th hole	343
8th hole	413	17th hole	507
9th hole	410	18th hole	473

This wonderful testing course ranks with the greatest in the game, and the present members, proud of their heritage, still enjoy staging golf's greatest events. The Walker and Ryder Cups, Open and Amateur Championships and all sorts of other major events have been played on this rather low-lying sandy links.

Royal Birkdale has everything for the big championships: a modern, functional clubhouse, a huge practice area, spectator mounds and extensive car parking facilities.

The club gained its royal status in 1951.

This course, which has two starting points, has also one of the most testing finishes in the game, players now having to negotiate 536, 401, 510 and 513 yards for the closing four holes of the championship round. The 6th hole was, in my experience, the toughest hole on the course; the alterations described by Bob Halsall make it a tremendous challenge.

Royal Birkdale is gradually losing its seaside fairways and greens. Today there are few really fast-running seaside courses left, and the Birkdale greens now hold almost every shot all the year round.

Mrs. Frances 'Bunty' Smith, one of our great lady golfers, is a member at Royal Birkdale, where J. A. A. Berrie's portrait of her hangs in the dining-room.

Visitors are welcome at Royal Birkdale, but an introductory letter is required.

Robert Halsall, professional, writes:

Founded in 1889 and, in fact, one of the oldest clubs in the North of England, Royal Birkdale has housed almost every major event in the game.

The club moved to its present site in 1897 and in 1931 the present modern clubhouse was built and the course was redesigned by Hawtree and Taylor.

The course, around 7100 yards now, is laid out in two loops of nine and it provides a challenging, but fair, test of golf, but the skill of its layout ensures that it can be enjoyed by tiger and rabbit alike.

New 5th and 6th holes are ready for the next championships and the sandhill between the tee and the green on the short 4th hole has been lowered to give a better view of the green.

You leave the 5th green, now a dogleg hole to the left played on dry sandy ground, and walk to the right well back, and from there you play down the narrow 6th fairway to the cross bunker. But as it is now 350 yards from the tee there is no chance of the 'Big Boys' carrying the lot, as they could from the old tee.

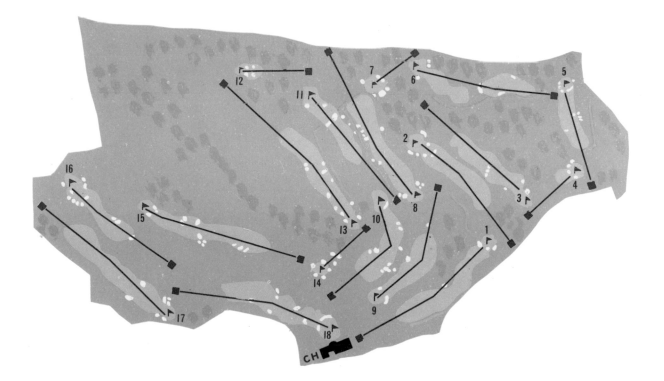

Royal Ashdown Forest Golf Club

Forest Row, Sussex

Tel: Forest Row 2018
Secretary: D. D. Grant-White
Nearest Station: East Grinstead
Nearest hotel: Ashdown Forest Hotel
Course record: 66 by H. A. Padgham
Visitors' fees: 20/– weekdays
                30/– Saturdays, Sundays and Bank
                Holidays

18 holes, 6210 yards

Old Course	yards	Old Course	yards
1st hole	300	10th hole	420
2nd hole	380	11th hole	240
3rd hole	315	12th hole	530
4th hole	360	13th hole	370
5th hole	500	14th hole	190
6th hole	130	15th hole	295
7th hole	330	16th hole	385
8th hole	480	17th hole	505
9th hole	150	18th hole	330

Here we have one of nature's golf courses, interesting and exciting, and of a type only to be found in our islands. There is no need here of artificial bunkering, for there are streams and pits and sandy roads, heather bordering every fairway and in the hollows which surround the greens to punish the bad stroke. Judgement of distance and the ability to keep a cool head among so much water, heather and gorse are both at a high premium. The course can now be stretched to 6500 yards, it is normally 6210 yards.

The clubhouse was built in 1893, five years after the club was opened, and very little alterations have been made to the original layout of the course. Hector Padgham, the club's professional, was one of the three Padghams who were assistants to John Rowe, who was professional to the club for 55 years and 1 day, until he retired in 1946. Two other Padghams learned their golf in this forest: Alfred Padgham, 1936 Open Champion, and Alfred H. Padgham.

The club has produced great golfers and has had some illustrious members, among them F. G. Tait and H. G. Hutchinson, Amateur Champions, and J. J. F. Pennick, a double winner of the English Amateur Championship; and from a host of artisan golfers came Abe Mitchell, our best professional never to win the Open Championship, and his half brother, Mark Seymour.

There is a second course on the same terrain, adjoining the Old Course. It is called, appropriately enough, the New Course, and is 6025 yards: a bit shorter and perhaps easier. Henry Luff, a former assistant of Fred Robson at Addington, developed it from a Ladies' nine-hole course. The clubhouse is the Ashdown Forest Hotel and here visiting societies have priority over members, even at weekends.

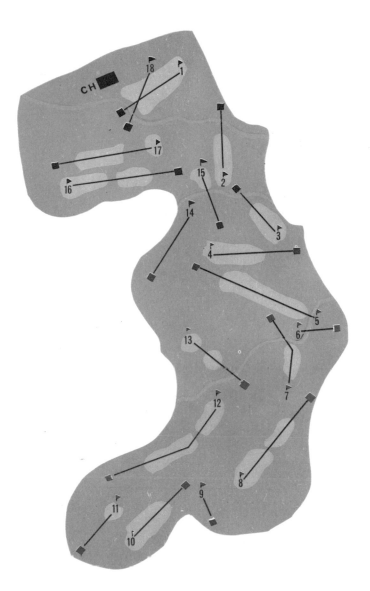

Hector Padgham, professional, writes:

I would describe Royal Ashdown Old Course as psychologically trying, with some intimidating carries for handicap golfers. For any player it is a course of character: the contours of the ground and the hard, tough turf make the player think out the shot to be played and then he must translate thought into exact execution, if the holes are to be taken in the figures with ease and comfort.

My best score for the course is 62, my eclectic 37. Recently I holed my second shot at the 5th hole of 500 yards, using a No. 2 iron; had four ones at the 6th, 130 yards, and one at the 14th, 190 yards: 5 in all.

I think the toughest hole is the 8th of 480 yards, playing it as a four, slightly uphill tee shot. The fairway slopes right to left and the green is guarded by a hump running from right to left, leaving a very narrow entrance on the left to the green. The prevailing wind is right to left. There is some difficulty in holding the ball up sufficiently to bounce the hump and yet not get caught in the heavy rough on the right. Most members, however, dread the 10th hole, a 420 yard steep uphill drive to a plateau green; many have difficulty in reaching this green in two shots.

Alwoodley Golf Club

Wigton Lane, Alwoodley, Leeds 17

Tel: Leeds 681680
Secretary: Ralph Middleton
Nearest station: Leeds, 5 miles
Course record: 68 by D. Fitton
Visitors' fees: Weekdays 10/— per round
15/— per day
Weekends 30/— per round or day
(15/— with member)
Weekly tickets £3

18 holes, 6755 yards

	yards		yards
1st hole	405	10th hole	476
2nd hole	308	11th hole	172
3rd hole	516	12th hole	372
4th hole	480	13th hole	396
5th hole	374	14th hole	211
6th hole	424	15th hole	415
7th hole	150	16th hole	439
8th hole	543	17th hole	435
9th hole	196	18th hole	443

Golf at Alwoodley, on a part of Lord Harewood's Wigton Moor estate, is a rare treat for the enthusiast who likes natural golf on land which nature might have designed specially for the sport.

Alistair McKenzie and architect A. S. Colt planned the original course in 1907. Some of Colt's greens are unaltered and still very tricky, some have been re-designed and there are new back tees at the 3rd, 4th, 6th, 8th, 10th and 14th holes. Originally 5692 yards, the course is now 6755 yards and it is, in general, narrow off the tee, as courses should be.

This is one of the great courses of that famous golfing county of Yorkshire and it has classical dog-leg holes.

The course really starts at the 3rd hole, after crossing a road which divides the course from the first and second par 4 holes. This road division would prove an obstacle to holding major events, with their attendant crowds, at Alwoodley. The 8th hole, 543 yards on the card and Stroke 1, is the most feared hole, a fairway curving to the left from the tee around a dangerously close wood has a formidable carry for the second shot; alternatively the player must find a narrow elbow of fairway.

As you leave the clubhouse, situated almost on the main Leeds–Harrogate road, and wander right out to the far end of the course, returning through dry, heathland turf, you are never far from the soot and bustle of city life. Yet there are few houses in sight and the tranquil beauty of these surroundings makes it seem a very different world indeed.

Alwoodley was, I suppose, the snob course of the area in its day, I do not remember any professional tournament being played there until 1967.

There have only been two professionals there in 60 years. The present professional is Ian Duncan, son of his famous Open Champion father, George Duncan, a local doctor. His predecessor, Jack Gandin, was one of the Guernsey band of professional golfers and a sweet swinger of a club, but with no golfing temperament for the major events. He was an institution at the club during his lifetime.

Ian Duncan, professional, writes:

A very interesting and fairly testing course, the character of Alwoodley is moorland, with plenty of heather, gorse, bushes, trees and consuming undergrowth. It is peaceful and perfect; we are still fortunate in not being encroached by new housing. We have, also, a good sized practice ground: 600 yards by 150.

Alwoodley was, for much of its existence, one of the most private clubs in the country, seeking no publicity and having no need to solicit membership. But in 1965, for the first time, we acted as host to the Yorkshire Amateur Championship, and the English Ladies' Championship was held here in 1967. Green fee-paying guests are now welcomed at the club on any weekday.

Moor Park Golf Club

Rickmansworth, Herts

Tel: Rickmansworth 73146
Secretary: Lieutenant Colonel C. L. Melville, D.S.O.
Nearest station: Moor Park, ¾ mile
Hotel: The Orchard Hotel, Ruislip
Course records: High Course 64 by E. C. Brown
West Course 63 by A. D. Locke,
A. Lees and
E. E. Whitcombe
Visitors' fees: Weekdays 30/– per day or round
(15/– with member)
Visitors not allowed at weekends

High Course, 18 holes, 6652 yards;
West Course, 18 holes, 6011 yards

	High Course yards	West Course yards		High Course yards	West Course yards
1st hole	372	340	10th hole	149	265
2nd hole	415	400	11th hole	396	326
3rd hole	162	337	12th hole	204	460
4th hole	438	170	13th hole	501	160
5th hole	337	405	14th hole	440	478
6th hole	491	130	15th hole	396	443
7th hole	363	465	16th hole	495	405
8th hole	466	390	17th hole	400	282
9th hole	477	245	18th hole	150	310

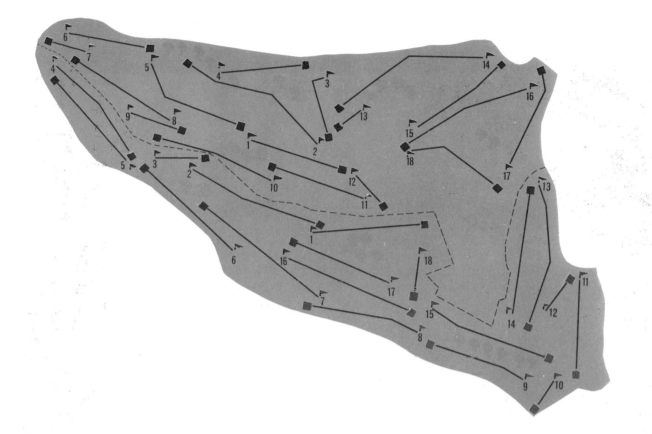

I risk no contradiction in claiming that no golf club in the world has such an imposing and historic clubhouse as Moor Park. The story of Moor Park goes back to the thirteenth century when it was called the Manor of More. Among its distinguished owners were Cardinal Wolsey and the Earl of Monmouth, and it is recorded that Queen Katherine of Aragon resided at Moor Park during the divorce proceedings. The present mansion was restyled by an Italian architect and contains some of the finest surviving work of the Venetian artist Giocomo Amiconi.

The club came into being as a member's club in 1937, but golf was first played there in 1923, four years after the estate was purchased by Lord Leverhulme.

The course is seventeen miles from London, situated on undulating parkland giving splendid views of the Hertfordshire countryside. It is an elegant course, with its majestic oaks and pines as obstacles, and it looks its very best in the early spring when daffodils make a riot of colour among the trees.

The great golf course architect, H. S. Colt, planned the 6652 yard High Course, and a splendid test of golf it is! Many major events have been held over this course, including the *News of the World* Match Play Championship, which I won there in 1932. Eric Brown holds the course record of 64. The shorter West Course is 6013 yards, and never easy to score on. The High Course is an 'out and back' layout, but the West Course has two starting points. I think the toughest hole on the course is the one shot 12th, 204 yards across a valley, because it has a double plateau green with a steep slope up to the narrow top ledge – a

green to three putt if the ball stops down below the hole. I felt that a '3' there was almost like a birdie, especially in the days when the greens were less watered than they are today.

One of my memories of Moor Park concerns an old friend, Vincent Lambourne, who had a gold-plated key made for his new locker, which he presented to me so that I could use his locker whenever I played there. When I took advantage of his offer, at the Silver King Tournament in 1937, he said: 'Its number, 279, will be your winning score.' And he was right!

Ross Whitehead, professional, writes:

The two courses at Moor Park – the High and the West – make a most enjoyable day's golf. This, I am sure, would be borne out by the very many visitors we have during a year who play the course in their Society meetings. The greens are of the very highest standard and once you have learned to read the subtle slopes on them there is no reason to miss any valuable putts at all.

It is a rewarding course to the player who can place his shots from the tee, this will give him a number of chances to pick up a shot on par.

I think that the hardest hole on both courses, from the point of view of professionals and club members alike, must be the 14th of 478 yards on the West course: a tee shot across a valley on to a fairway that slopes from the woods on the right to more trees on the left. The second shot, if you can reach the green, is over bunkers just short of the green that is tucked away behind the shoulder of a hill on the right.

Woodhall Spa Golf Club

Woodhall Spa, Lincs

Tel: 3111

Secretary: C. H. Caswell

Nearest station: Woodhall Junction, 2 miles

Hotels: Petwood Hotel, Dower House Hotel, Golf Hotel and Spa Hotel

Course record: 68, by E. B. Williamson

Visitors' fees: Weekdays 15/– per round
(10/– with member)
25/– per day
(20/– with member)
Weekends 20/– per round
30/– per day

18 holes, 6823 yards

	yards		yards
1st hole	358	10th hole	331
2nd hole	409	11th hole	447
3rd hole	416	12th hole	151
4th hole	409	13th hole	438
5th hole	155	14th hole	492
6th hole	500	15th hole	328
7th hole	414	16th hole	400
8th hole	198	17th hole	327
9th hole	557	18th hole	493

The sandy fairways of Woodhall Spa course, fringed by heather, gorse and broom, with silver birches as a background, is more characteristic of a course in Surrey or Berkshire than in Lincolnshire. This element of constant surprise is a considerable part of the charm of the course itself, which is one of the best inland courses in our islands and now, stretched to 6823 yards, a real test of golf. The professional record on the course is 68. It was originally planned by Vardon and Taylor in 1905, but was later completely reshaped by the owner, Colonel S. V. Hotchkin. Although the course has been altered from time to time, and crosses a railway line, it has the usual weakness of the 'out and back' layout; no two starting points.

The English Ladies' Championship, the Ladies' Home Internationals and the Brabazon Trophy have been held at Woodhall Spa. The English Amateur Championship was played there for the first time in 1967, by which time a valuable new nine-hole pitch-and-putt course had been added to the club's amenities.

The beauty, and perhaps also the biggest disadvantage of this ideal course is that it is far from a big town: nineteen miles east of Lincoln and the same distance from Boston and Sleaford. But I do enjoy playing on these dry, clean, sandy layouts, where the ball can be clipped off the turf without the need to take a huge divot.

Alf Fixter, professional, writes:

Situated in the very heart of the rich agricultural belt of Lincolnshire, Woodhall Spa golf club is far removed from the 'madding crowds' and provides golf of high quality: an unusual combination. It is a testing heather and sandy course, very good for winter golf, and said to be one of the best inland courses in the country.

I first joined the club as an assistant in 1933, becoming professional in 1938. Over the years I have collected an eclectic score of 41; the amateur and professional record score is 68.

Our greens are not too difficult and there are no trick slopes. I would say that the 11th, at 447 yards, is the toughest hole, being especially narrow; but the 500 yards long 6th hole is our number one stroke hole.

We have a very adequate practice ground a short way from the clubhouse. A recent and very attractive addition for members is the small tricky nine hole 'Pitch and Putt' course beside the clubhouse.

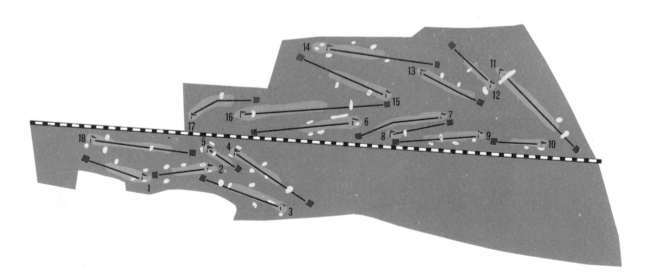

Burnham and Berrow Golf Club

Burnham-on-Sea, Somerset

Tel: Burnham 3137
Secretary: Lieutenant Colonel C. A. Burden
Nearest station: Highbridge — 2½ miles
Hotel: Queen's Hotel, Burnham-on-Sea
Course record: Professional, 69 by W. Smithers
Amateur, 67 by G. Irlam
Visitors' fees: Weekdays 15/– per round,
20/– per day;
Weekends 30/– per round or day
(20/– with member);
Weekly ticket £3, Monthly ticket £5.

18 holes, 6588 yards

	yards		yards
1st hole	387	10th hole	366
2nd hole	400	11th hole	426
3rd hole	390	12th hole	478
4th hole	485	13th hole	400
5th hole	158	14th hole	142
6th hole	435	15th hole	429
7th hole	447	16th hole	339
8th hole	482	17th hole	202
9th hole	165	18th hole	457

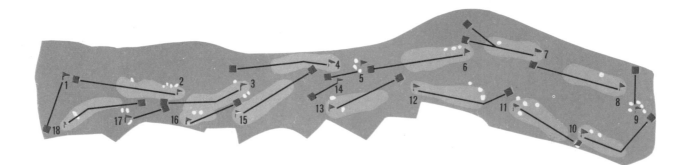

No architect could fail to make a good course on this piece of natural golfing terrain, but the first man who designed Burnham managed to fit in half a dozen blind short holes. Between 1918 and 1936 alterations were made to the 1st, 2nd, 4th, 9th, 10th, 13th, 14th and 17th holes, so that now the blindness has almost gone and the course, with its great sandhills and hard-to-strike greens, makes a fine test of golf.

J. H. Taylor, who was given his first chance as a professional at Burnham, said: "I was afforded a splendid opportunity of developing my mashie play at Burnham, for everybody who is familiar with it knows it to be one of the most sporting courses conceivable, with its large sandhills and small greens, necessitating very accurate approach play." A very clear assessment by a great golfer.

The turf on the shore of the muddy-looking Bristol Channel is glorious and there is no excuse for not hitting the ball truly to the greens from the 'pretty'. The course runs mainly north and south, so there must be days when, with a southwester blowing, the last nine holes will be tough on a slicer. The hardest drive of all is to hold the ball into a headwind coming a bit from the left . . . and there is no shelter at Burnham and Berrow.

This is great golf in a perfect setting, with the wide Bristol Channel to the left, the coastline of Wales in the dim distance and to the right the green and purple hills of Somerset.

Fred Bradbeer, professional, writes:

This is a testing seaside course as a range of sandhills runs along the righthand side of the first nine holes and again along the righthand side of the back nine, with rough grass on the other sides. Leave the fairways, which are on the narrow side, and you are in trouble.

I find it difficult to single out any hole as the toughest, for the wind always seems to be blowing across the course.

Burnham is a great test of golf. Although it is not easy, its charm increases the more you play it and its layout is so good that it is not unkind to moderate players who will be pleased to know there are comparatively few bunkers.

Royal North Devon Golf Club

Westward Ho! North Devon

Tel: Bideford 3824
Secretary: C. F. Stephens
Nearest station: Bideford — $2\frac{1}{4}$ miles
Nearest hotels: King's Head Hotel, Northam;
New Inn, Bideford.

Course record: Professional, 67 by D. Webster
Amateur, 65 by R. C. Champion
Visitors' fees: 15/— per round, 20/— per day;
Weekly ticket £3, Monthly ticket £6.

18 holes, 6543 yards

	yards		yards
1st hole	450	10th hole	344
2nd hole	424	11th hole	371
3rd hole	422	12th hole	425
4th hole	354	13th hole	440
5th hole	137	14th hole	178
6th hole	413	15th hole	410
7th hole	388	16th hole	145
8th hole	197	17th hole	548
9th hole	481	18th hole	416

This seaside course, steeped in golfing history, was founded over a hundred years ago by the Rev. I. H. Gosset and had originally twenty-two holes.

The fabulous Devon golfer, J. H. Taylor, learned his golf at Westward Ho. When he was houseboy in the home of Colonel Hutchinson he used to caddy for the colonel's sixteen-year-old son, H. G. Hutchinson, and this aroused Taylor's first interest in the game. Within a very few years he became the first English professional to beat the Scots at their own game as he won the Amateur and Open titles. Westward Ho paid a charming tribute to this winner of five Opens and a fine golfer for most of his long life when, in 1957, they made him President of the club at which he had caddied as a small boy. J. H. Taylor died at his native village nearby, in 1966, at the age of ninety-two years.

Scoring has never been low at Westward Ho. The Amateur, Ladies' and English Championships have been played here, but although this has all the requirements of a championship course its remoteness makes it unpopular with the authorities.

My own most vivid souvenir of Westward Ho is of the largest bunker in all England, if not in all golf, to be carried at the 4th hole. This is not much of a problem for the tigers but it must be frightening for the rabbit, with the sleeper face glaring up at him.

Stanley Taggart, professional, writes:

The oldest links in England, Westward Ho, celebrated its centenary in 1964. The course is mainly flat, there is no rough fairway and the greens are fast, real seaside ones, not puddings. Main features of this course are the sea rushes – sharp and tough enough to pierce a golf ball – fog, burns and hidden sand bunkers.

I think the 11th is our toughest hole: a drive over sea rushes with more rushes lining the undulating fairway. The second shot has to be played to a well-bunkered green with a slope on it.

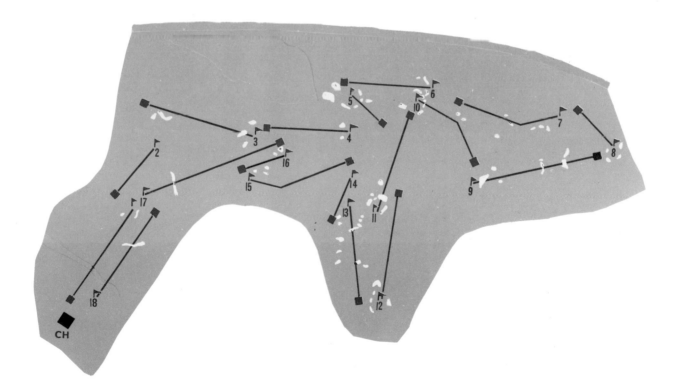

Parkstone Golf Club

St Osmunds Road, Parkstone, Poole, Dorset

Tel: Canford Cliffs 78025
Secretary: J. D. Bond
Nearest station: Bournemouth West – 2 miles by bus
Nearest hotel: Branksome Towers
Course record: Professional, 63 by Peter Alliss
Visitors' fees: Weekdays 20/– per round or day
(10/– with member);
Weekends 30/– per round or day
(15/– with member);
Weekly ticket £5.

18 holes, 6202 yards

	yards		yards
1st hole	354	10th hole	420
2nd hole	160	11th hole	510
3rd hole	490	12th hole	328
4th hole	275	13th hole	361
5th hole	373	14th hole	145
6th hole	494	15th hole	422
7th hole	170	16th hole	148
8th hole	327	17th hole	530
9th hole	505	18th hole	190

This fine course is Bournemouth's golfing pride and joy, for although the postal address of the club is Poole, Dorset, this prosperous club is sited amongst the luxurious homes of Bournemouth, that queen of southern towns.

Because of its sheltered position and the mild climate of this area, Parkstone is a very popular all-the-year-round course. It is picturesque too, with marvellous views over the Purbeck Hills and across Poole Harbour, and several holes skirt ornamental lakes graced by swans and wildfowl. Gorse, heather and birch trees make a blaze of colour in season and the course is protected from east winds by extensive pine woodlands.

Club professional Peter Alliss, a Ryder Cup player and one of our longest hitters, has scored a 63 on his own course, which is not surprising for someone with his golfing talent.

I have played at Parkstone a number of times and it has been worth the journey every time. Perhaps some of the holes are flattering, but club golfers get great satisfaction from picking up pars. Both long and short handicaps are rewarded at Parkstone with a wealth of different shots which keeps the course ever-changing and never boring.

The 190 yard 18th hole is no certain 3. You either hit the green, built cleverly into a steep heathery hillside, or else you set about scrambling for your 3 and will often be pleased to get out with a 4.

This is a holiday course where visitors are welcome and where every player, scratch or 24 or 36, will really enjoy his golf.

Peter Alliss, professional, writes:

Our greens are very good, easy to read and well watered in the summer by automatic pop-ups with water from our own lakes. We also have a small practice ground.

We cannot house big events which draw crowds, because we lack tent space, sufficient car parking area and practice facilities. But we have a very keen membership of eight hundred players always ready to bring the best golfers to Parkstone for exhibition matches.

I think our 11th hole from the back tee, the 520 yards uphill, is our toughest. The carry is 180 yards to the fairway; heather, trees and gorse line the fairway on both sides and there is a twenty-foot drop on the right of the green into real jungle country.

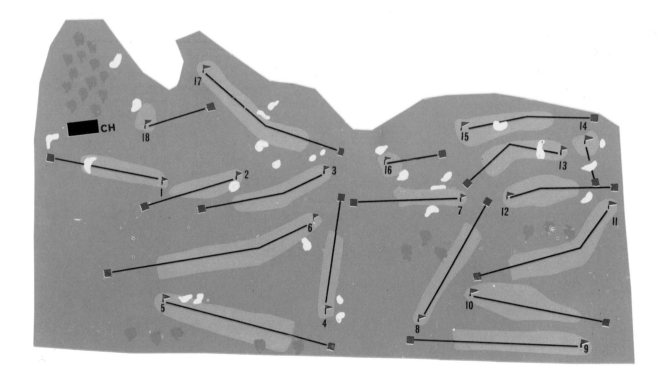

Fulwell Golf Club

Hampton Hill, Hampton, Middlesex

Tel: 01-977 3188
Secretary: R. Crosskin
Nearest station: Fulwell – 200 yards
Visitors' fees: Weekdays 25/– per round,
    20/– per day;
    Weekends 40/– (20/– with member).

18 holes, 6502 yards

	yards		yards
1st hole	380	10th hole	358
2nd hole	421	11th hole	510
3rd hole	340	12th hole	420
4th hole	290	13th hole	205
5th hole	482	14th hole	432
6th hole	155	15th hole	336
7th hole	400	16th hole	178
8th hole	460	17th hole	575
9th hole	160	18th hole	400

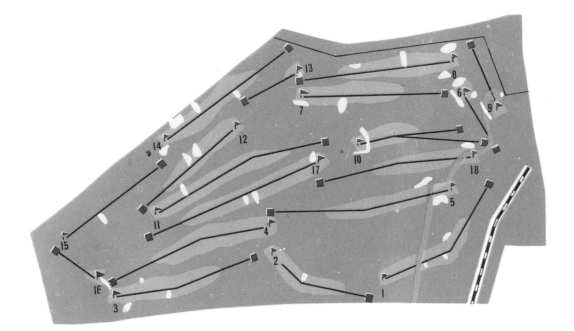

This London course is quite a test of golf.

J. H. Taylor designed the original course in 1904 and in 1950 J. Morrison planned the present one which is one of the most convenient courses I know, with an 18 holes ladies' running inside the large course. It is never easy to score at Fulwell as there is no help from the ground and no elevated tees.

I began my professional golfing career as No. 5 assistant to W. G. Oke, who was then the club's professional. I well remember dashing round the course trying to improve my game during my lunch hour and in the evenings. Another memory of my life as a 'dog's body' at Fulwell was of carrying round a two-foot length of lead pipe for weeks before I discovered that someone had pushed it into the bottom of my golf bag. Carrying the extra burden may have developed some of my muscles, but I failed to appreciate either this or the joke at the time.

The present professional at Fulwell, Bill Cox, was a former assistant of mine at Langley Park, Waterloo and Wimbledon Park, and is now a renowned golf instructor.

W. J. Cox, professional, writes:

Fulwell is a mixture of heath and park golf and one of the driest courses in the Home Counties. It is our boast that we never have temporary greens or tees and the course is seldom closed. Preferred lies are the rule in winter.

The 17th hole, 575 yards long, is one of the toughest holes in the country. This double doglegged hole ruins more scores than any other on the course.

Because some of the greens are exposed and others sheltered there is an understandable variation in pace, so the greens at Fulwell are never easy.

We are fortunate in having one of the finest practice grounds in the country, 300 yards long and over 100 yards wide. There is also a full size practice green and bunkers, and two large teaching shelters, which are a boon in bad weather.

West Sussex Golf Club

Pulborough, Sussex

Tel: Pulborough 2563

Secretary: B. L. H. Coles

Nearest station: Pulborough – 2 miles

Hotel: Arun Hotel, Pulborough

Course record: Amateur, 63, by David Harrison

Visitors' fees: Weekdays 30/– per round or day;
Weekends 50/– per round or day;
Weekly tickets £9.

18 holes, 6210 yards

	yards		yards
1st hole	459	10th hole	425
2nd hole	413	11th hole	445
3rd hole	375	12th hole	210
4th hole	355	13th hole	377
5th hole	144	14th hole	438
6th hole	230	15th hole	135
7th hole	450	16th hole	370
8th hole	181	17th hole	445
9th hole	349	18th hole	409

This heather and pine course, situated in peaceful open countryside just one hour's train ride from London, is a great test of golf.

An unusual feature of the design is the presence together of two short holes: the 5th and the 6th; these are fine holes, but as there are three short holes in the first nine this half of the course seems unbalanced and short.

Although there is not a single par 5 on the course and the longest hole is the 1st of 459 yards, and par is 67, a score under 70 at West Sussex represents good golf indeed. Amateur David Harrison's 62 is a very low medal round, but this is the sort of course where low scores can be achieved if the ball is kept on line throughout the eighteen holes, though deviations can be expensive and sometimes disastrous.

The toughest hole could be the 13th. It is only 377 yards, but the green is narrow and the hole runs uphill. If the flag is in the top righthand corner then the massive expanse of sand before the green has to be carried.

West Sussex is not an easy course to walk as there are a number of steep banks to negotiate. I remember having to give legless hero Douglas Bader a hand up some of the worst of them. On the flat this enthusiastic golfer is jet propelled.

Pat Keene, professional, writes:

This is a good golfer's course with hardly a dull hole. The fairways wander through heather, gorse, silver birch and pine trees, and the course itself is built on good golfing turf which always remains dry.

It is difficult to name the toughest hole; they are all good and bad shots are punished with equal severity. But the 6th and the 14th holes would be my choice as the most impressive holes on the course. About two-thirds of the direct line to the 6th hole is a marshy sort of scrub, culminating in a pond, and as this is an impossible carry for the longer handicap player there is an alternative way round on the right. The 14th is a superb hole of 438 yards. Standing on the tee you are faced with a long carry over heather and gorse bushes. Having avoided numerous bunkers there is a large slope falling away from the green which will carry your ball into long grass. There are trees to the back and to the right of this green, so the second shot to this hole has to be made with deadly precision.

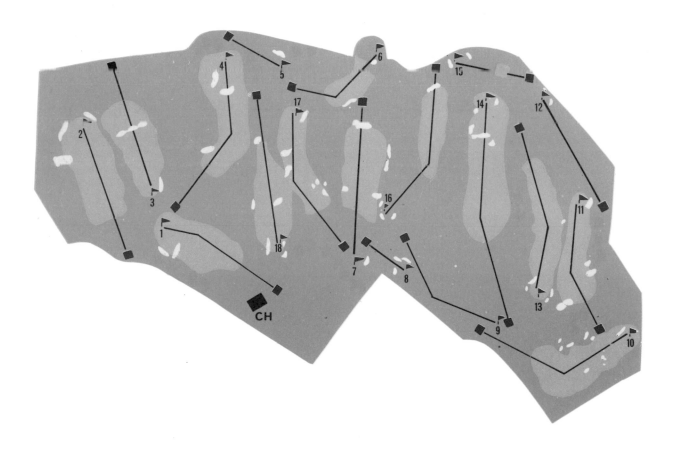

West Cornwall Golf Club

Lelant, St. Ives, Cornwall

Tel: Hayle 3319
Secretary: E. J. Roberts
Tel: Hayle 3401

Nearest station: Lelant – 5 minutes

Hotels: Porthminster Hotel, St. Ives;
Hendras Hotel, Carbis Bay.

Course record: Professional, 63 by J. A. Learmonth
Amateur, 65 by A. C. Rowe

Visitors' fees: Weekdays 12/6 per round,
20/– per day;
Weekends 25/– per round
(12/6 with member),
40/– per day (20/– with member);
Weekly tickets £3.10.0.

18 holes, 5671 yards

	yards		yards
1st hole	234	10th hole	272
2nd hole	373	11th hole	363
3rd hole	341	12th hole	475
4th hole	350	13th hole	255
5th hole	184	14th hole	416
6th hole	306	15th hole	140
7th hole	189	16th hole	500
8th hole	329	17th hole	194
9th hole	400	18th hole	350

Golf was started at Lelant by a cleric, the Rev. R. F. Tyacke, who probably learned his golf at Westward Ho! He saw that there was some fine golfing country at Lelant and, aided by some local enthusiasts, he quickly got a nine-hole course constructed. The site he chose was an ideal one for this true seaside course is splendidly situated.

One of the toughest holes on this course is the 500 yard 16th. As well as being long it is slightly uphill, and as the entrance to the green is not wide the player must achieve great accuracy.

Golfers will not easily tire of playing this course. Although not long as courses go, Lelant is not a course to be taken lightly, even a tiger will not find it easy to achieve a record score here.

J. A. Learmonth, professional, writes:

West Cornwall, splendidly situated overlooking St. Ives Bay, is a true seaside course with fine turf and large undulating greens which are very tricky.

The 2nd hole is one of the best holes on the course and is also the most difficult. This is a slightly right-hand dogleg with plenty of trouble on the right in the shape of some sandhills. The line is obviously to the left, for that direction opens up the green, which is elevated with a very narrow entrance.

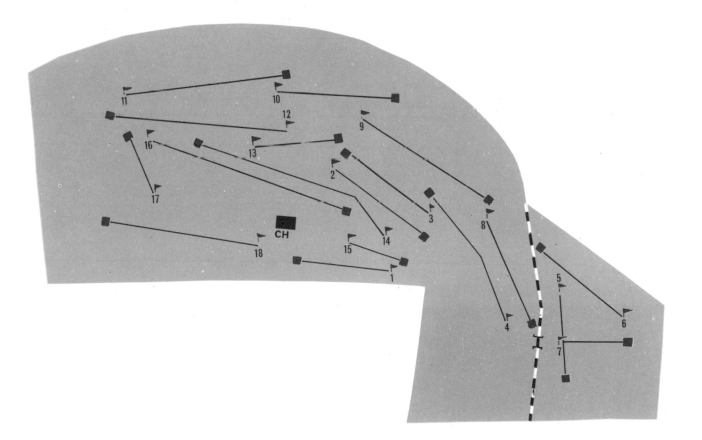

Moortown Golf Club

Harrogate Road, Alwoodley, Leeds 17

Tel: Leeds 686521
Secretary: J. A. R. Collinge
15 minutes bus service from Vicar Lane, Leeds, and Victoria Avenue, Harrogate
Hotels: Harewood Arms, Leeds, and many more in vicinity
Course record: Professional, 64 by B. Hunt.
Visitors' fees: Weekdays 15/— per round, 25/— per day.
Weekends and Bank Holidays limited to members and members' guests.

18 holes, 6604 yards

	yards		yards
1st hole	500	10th hole	556
2nd hole	464	11th hole	442
3rd hole	450	12th hole	168
4th hole	187	13th hole	418
5th hole	415	14th hole	164
6th hole	224	15th hole	396
7th hole	446	16th hole	447
8th hole	176	17th hole	364
9th hole	369	18th hole	418

This Yorkshire course, just five miles from the heart of Leeds, lies on peaty moorland, with plenty of gorse and heather, some silver birches and mixed spinneys, and some narrow streams as water hazards: a testing course of 6604 yards.

Moortown is an out-and-back course, like so many of the old layouts. The spongy peat provides fine turf, but many of the fairways have humps and hollows galore. I wouldn't consider the greens easy, but Bryon Hutchinson says "there are a few gentle slopes".

This club has been host to many *Yorkshire Evening News* tournaments, also the English and the Ladies' Championships. The first Ryder Cup Match was played there in 1929, when George Duncan's team beat Walter Hogan's team.

I always enjoyed going to Leeds and playing at Moortown when I 'did' the tournaments as a young man, because I felt that many nominated golf shots were demanded by this course. Holes like the dogleg 5th, of 415 yards around a wood, challenge the player to bite off as much as he dare in order to shorten the second shot. But the 418-yard 13th hole, with a wrist-high stone wall running along the left of the fairway's edge, is a real nightmare, for the ball must never have a draw on it or it will finish against the wall or, even worse, bounce over it.

My happiest memory of golf at Moortown is of hearing the roar of the crowd as I holed out from off the green on the 18th for a three – at the halfway stage of my Ryder Cup singles in 1929 – to go into lunch all square.

Visitors are welcome at Moortown, where they can enjoy a fine game on a course where history has been made.

Bryon Hutchinson, professional, writes:

The band of enthusiasts who founded Moortown Golf Club in 1909 chose their spot well. They saw the potentiality of a course of peaty moorland, much of which was under heather and gorse, fringed by a silver birch wood and intersected by streams. The original designer of the course, Dr. McKenzie, did a fine job in translating their ideas into a reality that is a superb test of golf.

I think the toughest hole is the 10th of 556 yards, which has a band of heather and scrub bisecting the fairway at 250 yards from the tee. All down the left and right sides of the fairway is more heather and scrub, and the green itself is well defended. This is a challenging hole for club golfers and professionals alike.

The professional record for the course is 64, held by Bernard Hunt. The amateur record of 67 is held by Alan Turner who, along with Alex Kyle, has been the most famous of our club amateurs.

Hunstanton Golf Club

Hunstanton, Norfolk

Tel: Hunstanton 2811
Secretary: Major E. S. Gates
Nearest station: Hunstanton — 1 mile
Hotels: The Neptune Hotel, Hunstanton;
        Le Strange Arms Hotel, Hunstanton.
Course record: Professional, 65 by M. E. Gregson
Visitors' fees: Weekdays 12/6 per round,
        20/– per day;
        Weekends 20/– per round,
        30/– per day;
        Weekly tickets £4.

18 holes, 6723 yards

	yards		yards
1st hole	347	10th hole	375
2nd hole	535	11th hole	446
3rd hole	445	12th hole	359
4th hole	158	13th hole	390
5th hole	423	14th hole	225
6th hole	336	15th hole	479
7th hole	164	16th hole	188
8th hole	493	17th hole	448
9th hole	515	18th hole	397

Hunstanton Golf Club has its home in a glorious stretch of natural golfing country at the top left hand corner of East Anglia, between the little river Hun and the sea. It is a fine test of golf for low handicap players and is an exciting adventure, not at all terrifying, for players in the higher handicap bracket.

Hunstanton has been the venue of many championships. The English Close Amateurs Championship has been played here three times: in 1930, 1951, and again in 1960 when Doug Sewell defeated Martin Christmas at the 41st hole after an epic struggle. The club has also been host to the British Ladies' Open Championship. Miss Cecil Leitch won her first Ladies' Championship here in 1914 after six unlucky years of failure and frustration, and since then the championship has been played three times at Hunstanton. Other major events which have been held here are the English Ladies' Close Championship, the Ladies' Home International Matches, the Brabazon Stroke Play Championship and the Schweppes Professional Championship.

A fine beach runs alongside the clubhouse and the area is well served with hotels, making Hunstanton an ideal choice for a family golfing holiday.

John Carter, professional, writes:

One never tires of playing this fine course. The texture of the greens has changed during the ten years I have been professional here; although it is still a links course one can see a more lush type of grass and softer greens emerging.

The club was formed in 1891 and George Fernie from Troon was responsible for the original layout over nine holes. This layout seems to have been on the easy side, but the extensions and improvements of the intervening years have changed all that and Hunstanton is now designed as a real championship test, though it is still not too severe a test for the holiday golfer playing the long two shotters at par 5.

I think the 445-yard 3rd hole is the toughest on the course. Here the tee shot is very important to set up the shot to the green. Playing into any kind of wind at all it becomes more a 4½ to 5 par. The short 16th must be one of the best short holes in Britain; it takes a good shot to earn a 3 here.

The official professional record is 65 by Malcolm Gregson in his final round of the Schweppes Professional Championship in 1967. The amateur record of 66 is held by Ronnie Shade. I have been round in 63 during the 1964 'Beat the Pro' contest. I remember playing with the late Jimmy Sherlock – professional to the club in the thirties – when he shot 83 round Hunstanton on his 84th birthday.

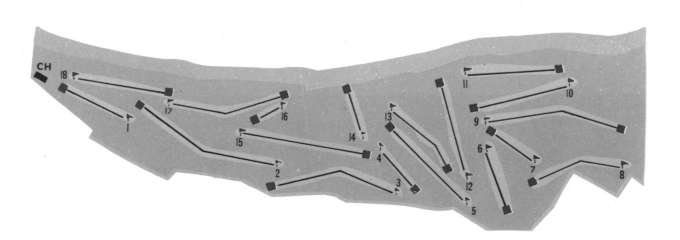

Temple Golf Club

Hurley, near Maidenhead, Berks

Tel: Hurley 248

Secretary: Commander L. A. Jeffrey, OBE, RN

Nearest station: Maidenhead, 3½ miles; bus service
from station

Nearest hotel: Aldingham House

Course record: Professional, 67 by K. A. MacDonald
Amateur, 66 by G. H. Micklem

Visitors' fees: Weekdays 25/– per day (12/6 with
member)
Saturdays 35/– per day (15/– with
member)
Sundays 40/– per day (20/– with
member)

18 holes, 6295 yards

	yards		yards
1st hole	367	10th hole	247
2nd hole	440	11th hole	431
3rd hole	358	12th hole	527
4th hole	494	13th hole	149
5th hole	151	14th hole	357
6th hole	412	15th hole	336
7th hole	342	16th hole	246
8th hole	229	17th hole	426
9th hole	514	18th hole	269

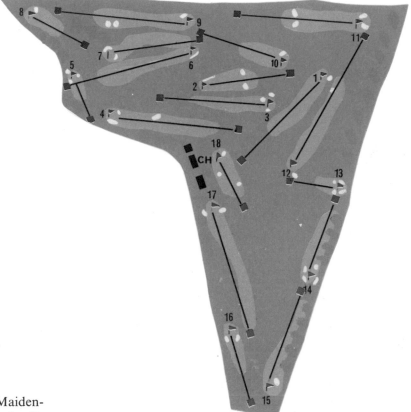

In the green belt, about midway between Maidenhead and Henley and sited among some of England's most beautiful countryside, lies Temple Golf Club, where I am the professional. It is on the main Maidenhead–Hurley road and just down the first section of the M4 motorway, thirty-three miles from London.

The layout is practically unchanged since Willie Park and J. Hepburn planned it in 1909. The course is tricky to score on, simply because no green is set up against the shot and so the ball goes forward off the pitch if incorrectly flighted and over-hit. There is only one starting point, but near the practice ground in the valley is the 13th tee where play can also begin on the rare crowded days.

The turf is superb at Temple and the fairway lies almost too good to be true; many of the trees on this wooded course are prize horticultural specimens. This is one of the few courses where electric buggies are allowed because little damage is done to this firm turf.

Temple is the home club of the Oppenheimers and Raymond Oppenheimer, following his father, is now the president.

Ashridge Golf Club

Little Gaddesden, Berkhampstead, Herts

Tel: Little Gaddesden 2244
Secretary: F. H. Sanders
Nearest station: Berkhampstead, 4 miles
Hotel: Bridgewater Arms Hotel, Little Gaddesden
Visitors' fees: Weekdays 20/— per round
40/— per day
Weekends 40/—
Weekly tickets £4

18 holes, 6453 yards

	yards		yards
1st hole	391	10th hole	355
2nd hole	494	11th hole	165
3rd hole	165	12th hole	405
4th hole	410	13th hole	476
5th hole	492	14th hole	376
6th hole	190	15th hole	513
7th hole	400	16th hole	167
8th hole	179	17th hole	482
9th hole	361	18th hole	432

Ashridge, with its enchanting valleys and stately trees, is a parkland course of unusual grandeur and variety.

The course was designed by the great triumvirate of golf architects, Major Cecil Hutchison, Sir Guy Campbell and Major Hotchkin, and although it is comparatively short it is still a fine test of golf and fun to play.

I know this course well, for I was professional at Ashridge from 1937 to 1943, and I have never tired of playing it.

The 9th hole is named after me, not because I designed it, but because of the way I played it. In favourable conditions, by hitting a drive which almost landed on a tablecloth at the end of the flight, the ball could be made to run on to the green 361 yards away. It needed some power in the shot to send the ball up the slope to the very much right-to-left sloping and slick putting green; while if it pitched too far it hit the steep face of the valley guarding the green. I did not reach the green every day, as can be imagined, but I drove on to it a number of times.

One of my memories of happy days at Ashridge is the superb playing condition of the course every day of the year. There was no weekend 'posh-up' here, and I am happy to say the standard has never faltered.

Alex Hay, professional, writes:

Ashridge is a wonderfully testing layout set into a forest which is preserved by the National Trust. A large herd of deer is often to be seen roaming about and the tree-lined fairways are a magnificent sight, particularly in spring and autumn.

The course spreads out from the clubhouse through the trees in a star shape, so that the wind seems to come from a different direction at every hole. There are very few bunkers in comparison with other courses, but the ones we have are so well placed as to be a continual nuisance. The greens are very long and somehow it is always one club more to the flag than you think.

One of the toughest greens to hit is the 9th, called 'Cottons'. This hole has proved so formidable that although only 361 yards long it is stroke 1.

The course record of 67 is held by Peter Townsend and was achieved in his last year as an amateur.

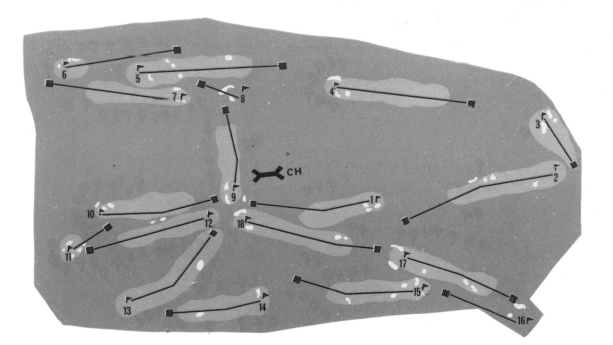

Sandy Lodge Golf Club

Northwood, Middlesex

Tel: Northwood 25429

Secretary: I. F. M. Lucas

Nearest station: Moor Park and Sandy Lodge

Hotels: Victoria Hotel, Rickmansworth;
Sportsman Hotel, Chorley Wood

Course record: 70 by A. Mitchell

Visitors' fees: Weekdays 20/– per round (10/– with member)
25/– per day (10/– with member)
Weekends 40/– per round or day (20/– with member)

18 holes, 6430 yards

	yards		yards
1st hole	500	10th hole	225
2nd hole	366	11th hole	547
3rd hole	151	12th hole	394
4th hole	479	13th hole	329
5th hole	412	14th hole	524
6th hole	465	15th hole	216
7th hole	234	16th hole	404
8th hole	105	17th hole	524
9th hole	398	18th hole	157

Sandy Lodge owes its existence to Francis J. Markes who, tired of playing winter golf on the sticky courses of North London, searched for a stretch of sandy subsoil and found all that he had hoped for at Sandy Lodge Farm, Northwood. The great Harry Vardon, Francis Markes' hero, laid out the course, which opened for play in 1910. This was again an out-and-back layout, for in those days no one thought of golf courses ever being crowded and of the consequent advantage of two starting points.

Francis Markes was a bit of a tartar. He kept the profits of golf ball sales for his club finances and discouraged the 19th hole drinking, but he loved Sandy Lodge and devoted his whole life to the development of golf there. He arranged many exhibition matches, which he loved.

An early 'gutta ball' match was Vardon and Duncan against Braid and Taylor, one pair using the gutta against the rubber in the morning and changing over after lunch. Braid and Taylor won by one hole.

After this match there was a long driving competition, which Braid won with 270 yards with the rubber core ball – that was over fifty years ago. George Duncan drove 240 yards with a gutta ball – some shot! Today's solid ball cannot be much better.

The stroke 1 hole at Sandy Lodge is the 11th of 547 yards, but I still find the long opening hole of 500 yards – with its huge sand bunkers just before the green – a real trial, especially for a golfer who has not had a proper warming-up session. To try to carry it or to play safe – the decision can make all the difference at this hole.

A feature of Sandy Lodge that I always remember is the 'shaved' greens, which Francis Markes proved without any doubt as being the only way to keep turf fine and firm. Other clubs might learn a lesson from this!

Bryan Patterson, professional, writes:
Sandy Lodge plays like a real seaside course, with sleeper-faced bunkers and rushes growing in prominent sandy areas. The fairways and greens are first class.

I find the short 10th hole can be tricky. The green is on a plateau, guarded by a deep sleeper bunker on the right and a pit on the left. From a range of 235 yards this hole demands some shot to get a comfortable par 3.

The par 3 holes at Sandy Lodge present the biggest problem for the members, for three of these holes are each over 200 yards long with smallish greens.

An extraordinary feat was achieved here by P. B. Lucas, who played blindfolded to hole the course in 85 – quite an achievement!

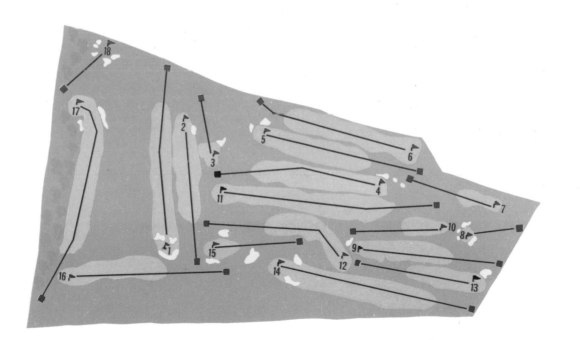

Notts Golf Club

Kirkby-in-Ashfield, Nottingham

Tel: Kirkby-in-Ashfield 3225 and 3380
Secretary: D. S. Robinson
Hotels: Black Boy Hotel, Nottingham, and others
Course record: Professional, 64 by E. C. Brown
Amateur, 67 by A. F. Bussell
Visitors' fees: Weekdays 20/– per day (10/– with member)
Weekends 30/– per day (10/– with member)

18 holes, 6931 yards

	yards		yards
1st hole	379	10th hole	356
2nd hole	426	11th hole	369
3rd hole	501	12th hole	438
4th hole	435	13th hole	227
5th hole	191	14th hole	410
6th hole	537	15th hole	445
7th hole	401	16th hole	341
8th hole	363	17th hole	480
9th hole	170	18th hole	462

Like many other famous old Golf Clubs, Notts was the brainchild of a parson, the Rev. A. H. Baynes. The course was designed by professional Willie Park Junior, who was considered the best 'holer out' of his day.

The surrounds of the course on one side – coal pits and their attendant slag heaps – seem out of keeping with the beauty of this dry heather and bracken heathland course, which I have always considered a wonderful inland course. The qualities of the course have not been overlooked by event organisers and many big tournaments have been held at Hollinwell.

Automatic watering has now been installed on the greens, but I hope they will not lose that firmness which I always associate with greatness. I have always considered the Hollinwell greens particularly difficult to read as the slopes are small ones.

Professional David Talbot – a fine golfer and winner of a major tournament – is only the fourth professional this club has had since its inception. Tom Williamson made history by going to Notts for a week's trial as professional and staying there until his death, fifty four years later.

One of the club's most famous members is Miss Enid Wilson, golfing queen of the early thirties and now a golf writer.

The Standard Scratch Score on this course is 74 – severe by any standard – but the holes are just as fair to the long handicap man as they are to the tiger.

David Talbot, professional, writes:

I would describe Hollinwell – which is the popular name for the club – as a severe heathland type of course: Played from the Championship tees it presents a formidable test for professionals and for the top amateurs; the Medal tees give a very interesting but slightly shorter course for the club competitions.

The course plays fast in the summer, but more growth on the fairways has tended to slow the course and make it play its full length.

There are two very good practice areas, one with five covered driving sheds which I use for teaching. Two new holes have also been added to the course to enable golfers wishing to play only nine holes to return to the clubhouse from the 7th hole via the new 8a and 9a holes.

Members find the 12th hole to be the most difficult, but I would nominate the 2nd, a left-hand dogleg with a slightly punchbowl green backed by a great fern-covered rock historically known as Robin Hood's Chair. The green is protected by two bunkers only, but they are strategically placed.

The best hole on the course is the 227 yard 14th, played from a high tee down a valley, at the foot of which is the green. The chief danger here is to underestimate the distance and be short.

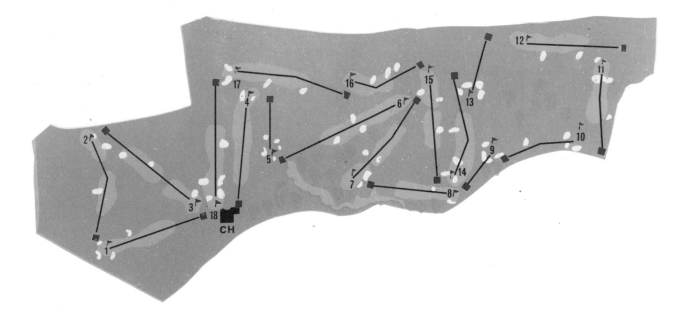

Formby Golf Club

Formby, Lancashire

Tel: Formby 4146
Secretary: F. Farey
Nearest station: Freshfield, 200 yards
Course record: Professional, 65 by N. C. Coles
Visitors' fees: Weekdays 30/– per day (10/– with member)
Weekends 40/– per day (20/– with member)

18 holes, 6862 yards

	yards		yards
1st hole	417	10th hole	521
2nd hole	390	11th hole	397
3rd hole	520	12th hole	430
4th hole	320	13th hole	391
5th hole	170	14th hole	423
6th hole	409	15th hole	414
7th hole	495	16th hole	130
8th hole	353	17th hole	478
9th hole	192	18th hole	412

Formby has a dual personality: part of the course lies on flat, rather dull, ground, and part of it lies on exciting golfing terrain with great sandhills. It is hardly a photogenic course, but with its stately pine trees, luscious turf, plateaux greens and dogleg holes, Formby is a course of character and a great test of golf.

Like so many courses of the last century – Formby was founded in 1884 – this is an out-and-back layout with, unfortunately, only one starting point. The twenty-four original club members erected a wooden hut with a thatched roof for their clubhouse. It was too small to include a bar among its amenities but legend has it that a bottle of whisky was kept under the floorboards to provide the members with liquid refreshment. The charge for a 'moderate go' at the bottle was threepence. Even when, in 1889, the membership had increased to seventy-eight, the year's bar profits only amounted to 14s. 8d. It looks as if a 'moderate go' wasn't specific enough to be profitable.

There is no adequate practice ground at Formby, but there is a charming and not too lazy ladies' course of 5417 yards running inside the big course. The ladies also have their own clubhouse, and this independent institution – a relic of the old days when ladies were not allowed in the clubhouse – is cosy and comfortable.

The original layout of the course has remained practically unchanged. One of the few new holes is the 170 yard 5th, to an elevated green sloping against the shot. Playing in a competition at Formby I got my only hole in one at this green – though I had played 16 holes already – and secured a cash prize. It was not one of those spectacular £10,000 prizes, only a modest £150; but it was still a nice reward for a perfect No. 5 iron shot.

J. M. Hume, professional, writes:

This great links, one of the many in that unique strip of sand dune country lying between Liverpool and Southport, has no longer real seaside fairways and greens; they are lush and green now, and very perfect. The fairway turf is, in fact, almost too good to play an iron from and take a divot – it would seem a sacrilege to do so.

There are two 18-hole courses at Formby, one of which is the ladies' course, which is completely encircled by the men's course.

The toughest hole on the course is the 12th. It requires a good drive, then a big and accurate second to reach the plateau green with its big bunker on the left. There is no way to scramble your second shot to this green.

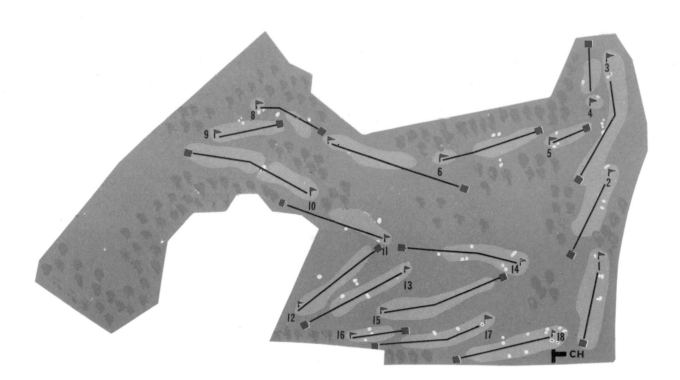

Yelverton Golf Club

Yelverton, Devon

Tel: Yelverton 3618

Secretary: H. G. Y. Jordan

Nearest station: Tavistock, 6 miles
        Frequent buses to and from Plymouth
        pass clubhouse

Nearest hotels: Moorland Links Hotel, Devon Tors
        Hotel and The Retreat

Course record: 65 by K. J. Hooker

Visitors' fees: Weekdays 10/– per round (7/6 with
        member)
        12/6 per day (10/– with
        member)
    Weekends 20/– per round or day
    Weekly tickets 46/6

18 holes, 6239 yards

	yards		yards
1st hole	208	10th hole	422
2nd hole	425	11th hole	404
3rd hole	170	12th hole	185
4th hole	315	13th hole	437
5th hole	477	14th hole	322
6th hole	145	15th hole	330
7th hole	442	16th hole	428
8th hole	573	17th hole	187
9th hole	286	18th hole	383

Yelverton is really Plymouth's golf course. Here wild ponies graze on the open common land, but they do not seem to damage the course. Indeed they provide a picturesque note that adds to the unique type of golf obtaining at Yelverton.

This course was laid out between the wars by Herbert Fowler and is almost untouched since he first plotted it as an out-and-back course. It is only 6139 yards but plays longer on the spongy moorland turf. During the war, when golf balls were in short supply, this course was widened considerably and the gorse and heather were cut back, but even now the fairways demand accurate striking from the tee to stay on them. Stroke 1 is the 442 yards 7th hole.

When you go to the West Country with your golf clubs look out for this unique course which has not, as far as I can remember, a single sand bunker, but has many hollows full of heather or thick grass – tougher bunkers really and much cheaper to maintain.

I have always enjoyed my visits to Yelverton. Although the main Plymouth to Tavistock road divides this course I have always experienced the feeling of being miles from everywhere when playing there.

K. J. Hooker, professional, writes:

Yelverton is an absolutely natural moorland course situated in the Dartmoor National Park some six hundred feet above sea level. There are two different types of golf on this course: the first eleven holes are played over undulating moorland and the last seven holes are much more broken up by old mine workings now grown over with gorse and heather making ravines and mounds.

I would describe the greens as being tricky, quite natural, often not built up at all and with many hard-to-read slopes. Our satisfactory practice area includes a practice green, but we do not have water laid on to the course.

There are several tough holes but I would single out the 13th as the most difficult and most members would agree. This hole measures 437 yards, with trouble each side of the fairway. To reach the green with a second shot one has to carry over a deep ravine with pits and hollows all round the green.

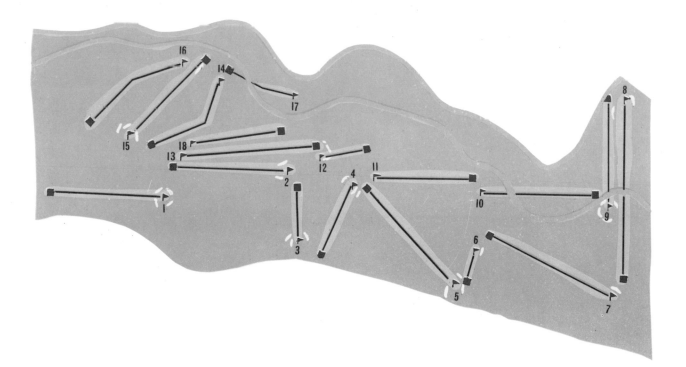

Coombe Hill Golf Club

Kingston Hill, Surrey

Tel: 01-942 2284
Secretary: K. A. Mackenzie
Nearest station: New Malden — 1 mile
Course record: Professional, 64 by Bernard Hunt
Visitors' fees: Weekdays, 30/— per round;
                Weekends, 40/— per round

18 holes, 6452 yards

	yards		yards
1st hole	328	10th hole	449
2nd hole	365	11th hole	425
3rd hole	425	12th hole	190
4th hole	476	13th hole	330
5th hole	488	14th hole	330
6th hole	185	15th hole	510
7th hole	356	16th hole	418
8th hole	428	17th hole	159
9th hole	187	18th hole	403

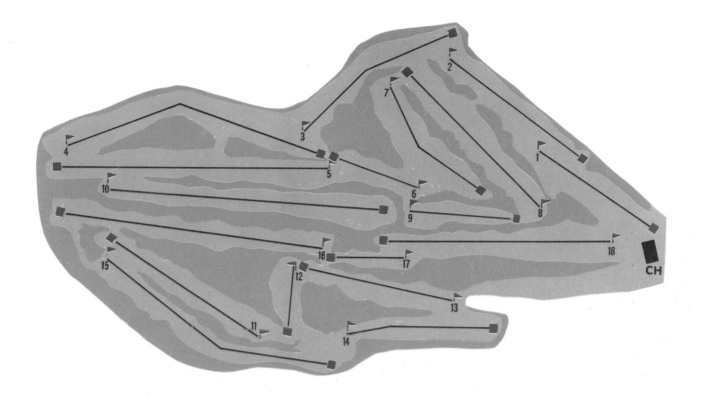

Here we have a beautifully designed course on sand and gravel, on rolling heath and heather parkland, with masses of rhododendrons forming evergreen backgrounds to many holes . . . and so near London, too!

This is one of the few courses designed by J. F. Abercromby, the founder of Addington Golf Club, and 'Aber' made a clever choice in selecting this site for another of his masterpieces.

The course is 6452 yards long and has perfect but tricky putting greens, so low scores without local knowledge do not come easily. There are two starting points, not too conveniently situated as the old 'out-and-back' idea was still the fashion when the course was planned. The absence of a practice area is compensated for by some excellent net practice facilities near the clubhouse. This clubhouse is, in my opinion, the best in the country, with a showpiece of a locker room on American lines.

Head greenkeeper George Hitchcock – son of the greenkeeper at Langley Park, where I had my first professional job – has been responsible for getting and keeping the course in such perfect condition. His son, Jimmy, a Ryder Cup golfer, grew up at Coombe Hill and received a lot of encouragement from the keen golfing members and from the professional, Richard Burton.

Dick Burton, 1939 Open Champion, is one of four Open winners to have been professional here, the others being Arthur Havers, Sandy Herd and myself. Archie Compston was also with the club for many years before going to Bermuda.

Dick Burton has scored a 61 once at his home course, but the official professional record is 64 by Bernard Hunt.

Visitors are welcome at Coombe Hill during the week, but the first tee is really crowded at weekends.

Richard Burton, professional, writes:
This heavily-wooded course is a first class test of golf, with well designed holes and every hole bordered by trees. One has to drive straight here and to place one's drives accurately.

The undulating greens are never easy to read, although the greens are now much slower and softer than they used to be, in keeping with the modern trend. In 1948 I was once just ten yards past the flag at the 8th hole when the ball slipped past the hole and ran twelve yards away, right off the green.

We have many difficult holes. I would pick out the 3rd, 4th, 8th, 10th, 14th and 18th as calling for especially good drives. Club members mostly dread the dogleg 3rd hole, 425 yards long to an elevated green.

Hankley Common Golf Club

Tilford, Farnham, Surrey

Tel: Frensham 2493

Secretary: Group Captain L. Martin

Nearest station: Farnham — 3½ miles. Motor buses from Farnham pass entrance to station and club

Nearest hotels: Frensham Ponds, Frensham; The Bush, Franham; Hog's Back Hotel, Farnham; Pride of the Valley Hotel, Churt

Course record: Professional, 63 by A. D. Locke

Visitors' fees: Weekdays, 20/— per round or day; Weekends and Bank Holidays, 30/—. 10/— per round or day for guests play-with members

18 holes, 6452 yards

	yards		yards
1st hole	505	10th hole	476
2nd hole	140	11th hole	220
3rd hole	350	12th hole	395
4th hole	324	13th hole	495
5th hole	305	14th hole	367
6th hole	540	15th hole	310
7th hole	180	16th hole	153
8th hole	507	17th hole	375
9th hole	375	18th hole	435

Hankley Common is an old club as golf clubs in England go, having been formed in 1895 by a band of enthusiasts who did much of the manual work in the laying out of the original nine-hole course. It continued to be a nine-hole course until 1922, when James Braid was called in to design a course of eighteen holes. Few alterations have been made to the Braid design.

The course lies in the 800 acres of Hankley Common, where the game is enjoyed against a background of heather, gorse, pines and silver birch trees: magnificent golfing country.

Bobby Locke practised a lot on this course, as it is near Farnham, where he stayed during his many visits to England in post-war years. He has scored a 63 there, while professional Keith MacDonald admits to a best of 64.

Keith MacDonald, professional, writes:
A 6452 yard long course on a very sandy piece of heathland with lovely open views, Hankley Common is one of the driest courses in Surrey. The greens are very good and of a very fine texture; they can be very fast, but once one has mastered the pace they are fairly easy to putt on.

The 18th is the most difficult hole as the second shot has to carry a ravine just short of the green and some 390 yards from the tee.

This course has produced two well-known lady golfers, Mrs. Elizabeth Price Fisher, who won the British Championship in 1959, and Ann Rampton, Captain of the English team in 1967 and 1968. Roger Wethered and his sister, Lady Heathcoat Amory, are life members.

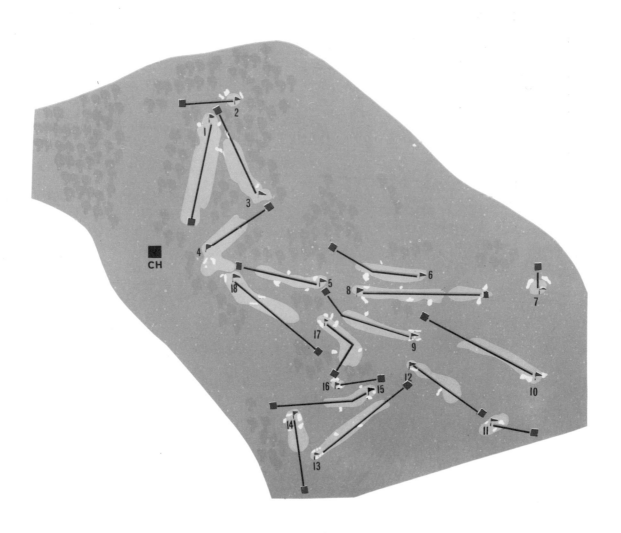

Liphook Golf Club

Liphook, Hants.

Tel: Liphook 3271

Secretary: Lieutenant Commander E. Dempster, R.N.V.R.

Nearest hotels: The Royal Anchor Hotel, Liphook; The Links Hotel

Course record: Professional, 69 by J. McGhee; Amateur, 69 by David Harrison

Visitors' fees: Weekdays, 20/— per day or round
Weekends and Bank Holidays, 30/—
£4 per week

18 holes, 6204 yards

	yards		yards
1st hole	215	10th hole	354
2nd hole	431	11th hole	167
3rd hole	133	12th hole	424
4th hole	478	13th hole	487
5th hole	484	14th hole	349
6th hole	433	15th hole	359
7th hole	161	16th hole	368
8th hole	349	17th hole	172
9th hole	431	18th hole	409

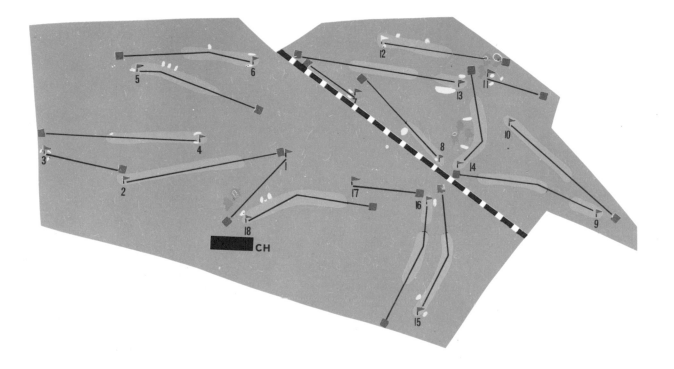

Here is a golf course in the famous Hants sand and heather belt, so good that even at 6204 yards it is testing by every standard. Trees line both sides of many holes and the sand bunkers are so placed that the ground area feeds them.

The Liphook greens are tricky and usually keen, this means it pays to get your shots to the flag on the easy side of the green with regard to the pin location.

Bobby Locke played a lot of practice rounds here when he lived here for half the year and he has a high regard for the qualities of the course.

A new clubhouse was erected in 1961 and it blends perfectly into the landscape. It is one of the later prefabricated types, which are both attractive and functional, as they can be readily enlarged.

J. A. McGhee, professional, writes:

Liphook is not a long course, but it is tree-lined and well bunkered, calling for accuracy rather than length. The fascination of the course is that the principal problem of almost every hole is produced by nature rather than by artifice

The club was founded in 1922, when the course was designed by A. C. Croome and T. Simpson. New 1st and 18th holes were designed by J. S. F. Morrison in 1946.

I hold the professional records of 69, official, and 65, unofficial, and my eclectic score, built over twelve years at the club, is 44.

The 6th hole, of 430 yards, is extremely tricky. A well-placed drive has to be followed by a particularly accurate iron shot to a green bunkered on both sides and with a deep hollow immediately behind the double-tiered green. Only the bold player can expect a three here. The 487 yard 13th is probably the most difficult hole for the handicap player. The drive has to be well hit if the broad ditch dividing Hampshire and Sussex is to be carried with the second shot. The player who has been forced to play short is faced with an iron shot from a hanging lie to an elevated, fast green to obtain his par 5. It is a magnificent hole, with a geographical peculiarity to give it added interest: you drive off in Sussex and hole out in Hampshire.

St Andrews Golf Club

St Andrews, Fife, Scotland

Course records:

Old Course: Amateur, 67 by Joe Carr.
Professional, 66 by Peter Allis,
B. J. Hunt and J. Nicklaus.

New Course: Amateur, 67 by Joe Carr.
Professional, 63 by F. Jowle.

Eden Course: Amateur, 65 by R. D. B. M. Shade.
Professional, 64 by W. McHardy.

Visitors' fees:

Old Course: Weekdays 12/6 per round;
Saturdays 20/— per round.
No play Sundays.

New Course: Weekdays 6/— per round;
Saturdays 8/6 per round;
Sundays 10/— per round.

Eden Course: Weekdays 6/— per round;
Saturdays 8/6 per round;
Sundays 10/— per round.

Jubilee Course: Weekdays 3/— per round;
Sundays 10/— per round.

Length of Old Course: 18 holes, 6581 yards

	yards		yards
1st hole	374	10th hole	318
2nd hole	411	11th hole	170
3rd hole	350	12th hole	312
4th hole	430	13th hole	402
5th hole	522	14th hole	513
6th hole	374	15th hole	398
7th hole	359	16th hole	351
8th hole	163	17th hole	466
9th hole	310	18th hole	358

There are four 18-hole courses on the St Andrews links, all of which are open to visitors: the Old Course, the New Course, the Eden Course and the Jubilee Course. The courses are under the management of a joint links committee representing the Town Council and the Royal and Ancient Golf Club. Sunday play is permitted except on the Old Course.

St. Andrews is the mecca of golf. All golfers dream of playing on the famous Old Course which begins and ends alongside a row of private houses, grey clubhouses and hotels.

Situated on the coast of Fife, on flat rather dull land where the sand bunkers – many made by sheep sheltering from the biting east winds – are out of sight, St. Andrews photographed from ground level scarcely looks like a golf course at all. Nevertheless this is, I suppose, the most famous golfing centre in the world. Golf has been played here for at least four hundred years and the Royal and Ancient Golf Club was formed here in 1754. King William IV granted the club royal patronage in 1834.

There are now four courses at St. Andrews: the Old, which is the course where the Championships are decided; the New, the Jubilee and the Eden.

The Old Course is different from any other course and is sometimes an acquired taste with newcomers. The great Bobby Jones called it a cow patch after his first time round. Later he acclaimed it the greatest golf course of them all and said it was the spot he would choose to live if he were obliged to live on a golf course.

There are seven tremendous double greens some hundred yards wide on this course today, with two holes on each green and some awesome bunkers with centuries-old names. The Beardies, Hell, Strath and the Principal's Nose are golfing household words.

The Old Course can, in fact, be played backwards, which is perhaps unique in the golfing world. There are only two short holes, the 8th and the 11th in what is known as the Loop, a series of shortish holes where all the low scores are built up. Slices are punished on this course, it pays to hook every time.

There is a new hotel now in the old station yard on the right of the famous 17th hole. This has altered the vista from the tee. With the infamous black sheds also gone and the bank of the green and the footpath beyond it made easier, the terrors of this hole have unfortunately vanished, for this was the killer hole at St. Andrews in its day: the scene of endless tragedies.

I think the toughest hole is the 567 yards 5th hole – a par 5 to a high green – but disaster lurks at many holes on this fine course.

The Open Championship is regularly held at St. Andrews and since a suggestion I made in prewar days was adopted – to rope in all the course and make it a golfing arena – St. Andrews is now, spectatorwise, the most modern course, for the crowds can follow the stars round the course from the side tracks and the spectator mounds.

I have played many times on this course and have broken 70 several times in tournaments; the record is 66. One of my outstanding memories is of seeing big Jack Nicklaus hit his tee shot with a 4 wood – for safety – four times on to the 18th green, a Championship drive of 381 yards.

Millions of golfing feet have trodden these fairways and greens over the years and while some parts of the course are in danger of losing their real seaside quality the greens and fairways have stood up well to the punishment.

Visitors are welcome to play on these famous links, but they can use the clubhouses only if introduced by a member.

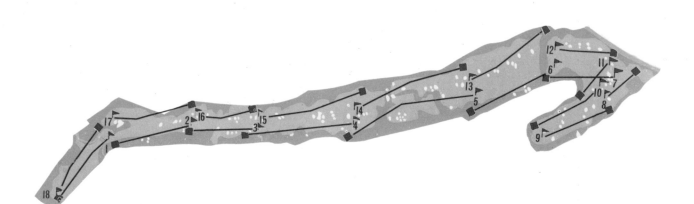

Gleneagles Hotel Golf Courses

Perth, Scotland

Tel: Auchterarder 2231

Secretary: J. F. Gordon, The Dormy House, Gleneagles
Hotel Golf Courses, Perth

Nearest station: Gleneagles, 1 mile. Buses meet all
trains.

Course records: King's Course, 64 by J. Adams
Queen's Course, 65 by E. C. Brown

Visitors' fees: Weekdays 27/6 per day in summer
12/6 per day in winter
Weekends 40/– per day

King's Course, 18 holes, 6644 yards
Queen's Course, 18 holes, 6055 yards

	King's yards	Queen's yards		King's yards	Queen's yards
1st hole	370	415	10th hole	457	418
2nd hole	405	156	11th hole	212	333
3rd hole	393	416	12th hole	402	438
4th hole	478	360	13th hole	465	150
5th hole	171	183	14th hole	285	230
6th hole	474	430	15th hole	465	266
7th hole	455	483	16th hole	151	382
8th hole	175	326	17th hole	390	213
9th hole	422	421	18th hole	474	435

Three superb courses to test any golfer's skill; turf that is springy and alive; greens groomed to manicured perfection and surroundings of Scottish scenery at its breathtaking best: this is Gleneagles, and what more could any golfer ask? Gleneagles *is* golf, and golf at its richest and loveliest.

There are three courses at Gleneagles: the King's, the Queen's and the Wee Course, a light-hearted nine-hole course which has its own special merit and quality. All holes on the three courses have names that are, for visitors, an education in the Scots language.

Both the big courses are out-and-back, so be prepared for an exciting long walk over the moorland ridges, from which the views are superb, especially the view up Glen Devon of which a local wag said, "If you can see the Glen it is going to rain; if you can't see it, it is raining."

Of the three courses I prefer the King's, the biggest of the three and a flattering course in many ways with its wide fairways and elevated tees, but no pushover with a card and a pencil.

James Braid plotted the courses before the First World War, but they were not opened until 1919 and the Gleneagles Hotel – the Savoy of the Highlands – opened in 1924. No flowery compliments can exaggerate the merits of this hotel; the pride of our islands, it has no peer and few equals in the whole golfing world.

All sorts of golfing events and television matches have been staged at Gleneagles, and why not? – it is such a treat even to stay in this hotel, and golf promoters, too, appreciate its merits.

There is land here for yet another superb course and with the popularity of Gleneagles increasing so deservedly every year this development seems inevitable.

Gleneagles is internationally renowned and attracts each year golfing pilgrims from every country in the world where the game is played. If you are a golfer and have never played at Gleneagles you are missing something special – do let me persuade you to take a look at this golfing paradise.

Ian Marchbank, professional, writes:

Fifty thousand rounds of golf are played at Gleneagles each year, yet the layout of our course ensures that each hole is played as it were in its own compartment or valley so that golfers enjoy a sense of complete privacy and seclusion.

The three courses at Gleneagles are of an undulating moorland type, excellent in every aspect and never muddy or wet. The greens are very tricky, but fine in texture and in perfect order. They are extremely large and well bunkered.

Designed by James Braid, one of the greatest British golf architects, and Major C. K. Hutchison, the courses lie on a moorland plateau 500 feet above sea-level in the heart of Perthshire.

I think the most difficult hole is the 13th on the King's Course which is appropriately, almost reverently, named 'Braid's Brawest'. Here the tee-shot has to carry a ridge, in the face of which lie two large bunkers. Unless the wind is very kind indeed only a perfect drive will serve, and even after playing such a drive the golfer is left with a long shot to a green lying on top of a small plateau – an entrancing target. For many visitors and members No. 13 has been a number of ill omen.

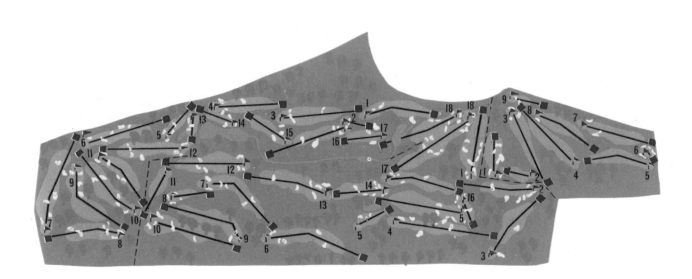

Muirfield Golf Club

Gullane, Scotland

Tel: Gullane 2123
Secretary: Captain Hanmer
Station: Drem – 4 miles
       Bus from Edinburgh takes 50 minutes
Course record: Professional, 65 by P. J. Butler
       Amateur, 70 by B. M. Shade

18 holes, 6806 yards

	yards		yards
1st hole	453	10th hole	480
2nd hole	353	11th hole	359
3rd hole	382	12th hole	380
4th hole	192	13th hole	153
5th hole	510	14th hole	458
6th hole	458	15th hole	393
7th hole	157	16th hole	193
8th hole	455	17th hole	513
9th hole	490	18th hole	427

The home course of the Honourable Company of Edinburgh Golfers is a superb tract of seaside golfing on the shores of the Firth of Forth and is one of the world's great tests of golf.

This is not a seaside links course in the true sense, but it enjoys many of the features associated with such courses: it is very heavily bunkered, the soil is light and sandy and dries out remarkably quickly and a wide expanse of sand dunes stretches down to the sea from the northern boundary of the course.

The club is recorded in golfing history as having been created in 1774, yet the club rules date from 1751 and the club was concerned in 1754 with forming the first set of Royal and Ancient Rules.

Muirfield became the home of the Honourable Company of Edinburgh Golfers on 2nd May 1891 as a sixteen-hole course. Later it was extended to 18 holes, in time for the Open Championship which was played there for the first time in 1892 and won by Harold Hilton. The next Open held at Muirfield was in 1896 over a new extended course, and this was won by Vardon after a tie with J. H. Taylor. Further extensions and alterations to the course have taken place over the years.

I have never discovered who designed this course, but it is perfectly planned with two well-balanced halves and the unique turf-faced sand bunkers are well placed and are a feature of the layout because of the steepness of their faces. In Muirfield it is a question of getting out first time and not going for length. The short holes here are full of character, the sort of holes that even the best golf architects would find difficulty in reproducing. The course has two starting points, which I always think makes playing and spectating a real pleasure, and the practice ground is of noble proportions. The condition of Muirfield, which is one of the few underplayed courses in our islands today, is always superb.

I think that the 9th hole of 500 yards is the toughest of many testing holes at Muirfield. With the green running away from the player and almost touching a chest-high stone wall on the left side, the dangers are not over even if the tee shot has been steered to the fairway, for it is not unknown for a ball to hop the wall or remain close to it, both of which could be tragic for a medal score.

I first played at Muirfield in Walter Hogen's 1929 Open and I enjoyed the first two rounds with him as partner, a lifelong happy memory. I have a very special affection for the course as it was here that I won my third Open Championship in 1948 when I made a course record of 66. King George VI watched play, after having wished me luck at the first tee; so it was indeed a royal occasion for me.

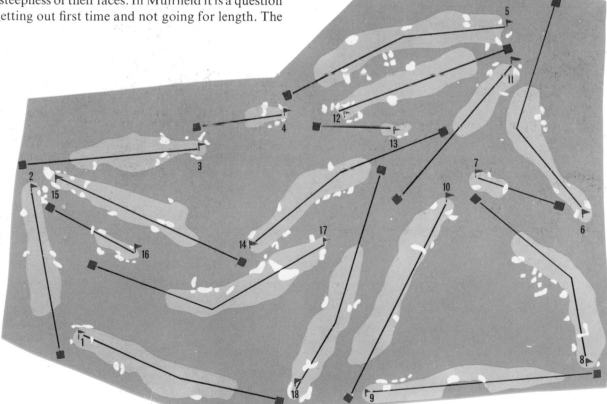

Carnoustie Golf Club

Angus, Scotland

Starters Box Telephone: Carnoustie 3249

Secretary: E. Kerr, Town Clerk, Council Chambers, Carnoustie

Tel: Carnoustie 3335

Two courses – Championship Course and Burnside Course – 18 holes each, owned and managed by the Town Council of Carnoustie

Hotels: Many available nearby

Course record: 67 by E. C. Brown

Visitors' green fees for Championship Course:
7/6 per round; 10/6 per day; 35/– per week

Visitors' fees for Burnside Course:
5/– per round; 7/6 per day; 25/– per week

Sunday golf on both courses, visitors' fees:
15/– per round; 25/– per day

Championship Course **18 holes, 7252 yards**
Burnside Course **18 holes, 6826 yards**

	Championship yards	Burnside yards		Championship yards	Burnside yards
1st hole	406	401	10th hole	446	406
2nd hole	468	448	11th hole	370	367
3rd hole	343	321	12th hole	473	476
4th hole	429	375	13th hole	168	145
5th hole	389	377	14th hole	485	487
6th hole	565	521	15th hole	460	424
7th hole	386	376	16th hole	243	235
8th hole	163	149	17th hole	458	438
9th hole	475	427	18th hole	525	453

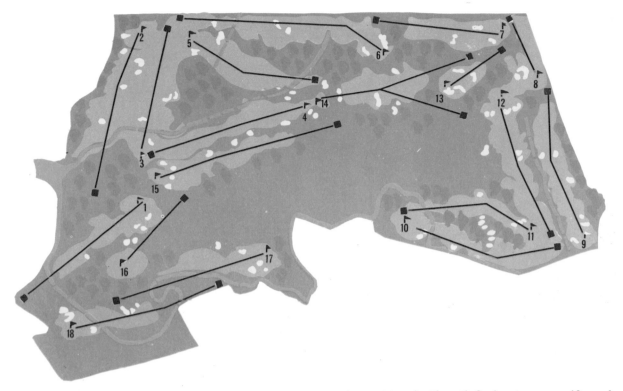

I have every reason to love Carnoustie because I won my second Open Championship title there in 1937, against very strong opposition and despite terrible weather conditions on the final day. So far only four Opens have come to Carnoustie, but I do not think it will ever leave the rota again, following the success of the 1968 'Player's Open'.

This course, on links land, has everything to make a searching golf test: length, huge greens, a frequent out-of-bounds fence, a winding burn and fickle weather. Now over 7100 yards long, the course was altered by James Braid in 1926 and lengthened a little. Golf, it is reckoned, was played on this ground long before the Carnoustie Club was formed in 1842.

The burn, 25 feet at its widest, winds about all over the course and has to be crossed seven times. Holes run in all directions, just to make life more complicated. Indeed, in this 'out and back' layout no golfer can afford to get slack with his thinking.

The 10th hole proved to be the toughest in the 1968 Open, statistically because of the narrowed down fairway and the constant head-on breeze bringing the nest of righthand traps into play from the tee. The fairway traps at tee shot length find out many golfers who consider themselves good drivers; punishment at this point on a golf hole is often disastrous, and there is plenty of this at Carnoustie.

If Gary Player can think well of any golf hole at Carnoustie it must be the 480 yard 14th hole. Here, two huge, round, deep sandtraps, cut into the face of a low sandhill, have to be carried to reach the green in two shots; they appear from the tee shot like spectacles. Gary got two eagles out of four tries at this hole, in the final round he picked up three shots on Billy Casper, who was leading at that moment, for with an out-of-bounds drive Casper ended with a 6.

Golf has made the town of Carnoustie world famous. Over three hundred of its players became professionals, pioneering and teaching the game far from home. In the process they won the Open Championships of Britain, America, Canada, Australia and South Africa. In Carnoustie, golf is more than a game; it is a way of life. Perhaps the best golfer of all the locals was Macdonald Smith, who made golfing history in the United States but never won the U.S. Open title.

There is no professional at Carnoustie; the course is built on ground held in trust by the Town Council and managed by a local Course Committee.

Visitors are welcome here, and if you fancy yourself as a golfer just try this course from the championship tees. My happiest souvenir of Carnoustie is playing the four rounds of the Open without a six on the cards.

Turnberry Hotel Golf Club

Turnberry, Ayr, Scotland

Tel: Turnberry 202

Secretary: J. McL. Barclay
Tel: Terminus 01 Ter 8822

Nearest station: Girvan Station, 5 miles

Course records: Ailsa Course — Professional, 67 by D. J. Rees
Arran Course — Professional, 69 by D. J. Rees, D. Thomas and D. J. Hunt

Visitors' fees: Weekdays, hotel residents ·10/— per round, non-residents 20/— per round
Weekends, hotel residents 12/6 per round, non-residents 30/— per round
Weekly tickets for residents 50/—
Fortnightly tickets for residents 70/—

Ailsa, 18 holes, 7060 yards
Arran, 18 holes, 6350 yards

	Ailsa yards	Arran yards		Ailsa yards	Arran yards
1st hole	365	380	10th hole	460	165
2nd hole	440	505	11th hole	180	315
3rd hole	475	160	12th hole	395	460
4th hole	170	330	13th hole	385	445
5th hole	490	425	14th hole	440	395
6th hole	245	390	15th hole	220	340
7th hole	520	230	16th hole	415	370
8th hole	440	390	17th hole	515	215
9th hole	475	455	18th hole	430	380

Turnberry is one of the great golf centres of the world. Here are two championship-quality seaside courses, many holes of which lie right on the shore, plus an excellent hotel – part of our British Transport group – which overlooks the golf holes and the sea.

Looking down from the hotel you can see the first nine holes of the Ailsa Course following the shore out to the white lighthouse on the Point, while over on the left Ailsa Craig juts out of the sea. The Isle of Arran rises up from the sea on the right and on a warm summer's day, with a heat haze on the velvety greens, the larks singing and the gorse in bloom, this could be a little corner of heaven on earth.

The Ailsa is the more popular of the two courses at Turnberry because of the spectacular tee shots from the dunes and rocks on the outward half, and because of the fascination of the tee on the top of the rocks at the 9th hole; a false step here can land the golfer in the waves breaking on the rocks below – definitely no place to drive off from if you suffer from vertigo!

Like Gleneagles and Moretonhampstead the hotel courses at Turnberry are really public courses de luxe. Although there are members with official club handicaps and regular competitions to play for, visitors and especially hotel guests have equal status with the local and regular golfers.

Many important events have been played here, including the Walker Cup, and the *News of the World* Matchplay Championship, and these events have always produced first-class winners.

There are practice facilities and even a difficult pitching and putting course right in the hotel grounds, but the extensive practice putting green is on too much of a slope to be useful for checking your stroke on.

I have played at Turnberry many times and I always find that the 5th is the toughest hole for me – the green is so hard to find with the second shot, even for the stars. This is a 500 yards par 5, with danger everywhere and some of the toughest rough I have ever tried to play from, which engulfs your ball if you fail to make the carry with your shot to the green from the left side of the fairway.

Robert S. Jamieson, professional, writes:
There are two superb courses at Turnberry, the Ailsa and the Arran. The Ailsa is a supreme links course. It is a driver's course with fairways which are not too undulating and all greens visible for second shots, which I consider essential to any great course. My best round over the Ailsa is a 63. Some years ago Mr. and Mrs. G. Gordon from Ayr halved the 11th in 1, each playing 7 irons.

The 15th short hole is, in my opinion, the finest hole on this course – it plays one of two clubs longer than it looks. Guarded on the left by three cruel bunkers and with a deep ravine running from the left round to the right corner there is only one place to play the ball and that is the green, or your par 3 can turn into a certain 4 or 5. Gene Saroyen has named our 9th as one of the greatest par 4s in the world. This hole requires a long accurate tee shot playing the second 3 to 5 iron into a narrow undulating green – the hole is so demanding that it does not have one bunker on it!

We have possibly the finest practice area in Scotland – two complex holes 425 yards long by 150 to 180 yards wide – and this may well be developed into a driving range in the near future.

We have a good number of caddies – many of them local characters such as Long John, The Wasp, Happy and The Lawyer. Once when Long John was caddying for an American visitor on the 9th hole he was asked if the lighthouse, visible from this hole, worked. His reply was "Yes, sir – but only at night!"

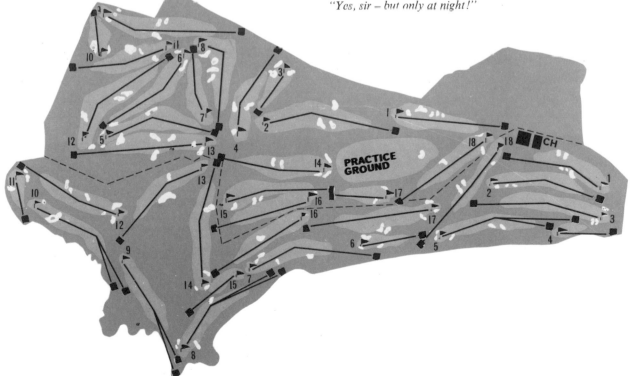

The Dalmahoy Golf Club
Dalmahoy, Kirknewton, Midlothian, Scotland

Tel: Ratho 343
Secretary: Squadron Leader G. R. Clark
Tel: Ratho 439

Situated approximately 7 miles from Edinburgh on the A71.

Buses from St. Andrews Square pass entrance to course.

Hotel accommodation available at Clubhouse

Visitors' fees: East course: Weekdays 10/– per round (3/– with member); 20/– per day. Weekends 27/6 (7/6 with member). West course: Weekdays 7/6 (3/– with member, 15/– per day. Weekends 17/6 (5/– with member).

East Course record: 65 by N. Coales and J. R. M. Jacobs

East course, 18 holes 6677 yards; West course, 18 holes 5297 yards

	East yards	West yards		East yards	West yards
1st hole	500	364	10th hole	500	172
2nd hole	422	281	11th hole	408	364
3rd hole	418	124	12th hole	440	338
4th hole	428	380	13th hole	145	543
5th hole	475	320	14th hole	340	343
6th hole	155	272	15th hole	398	130
7th hole	430	260	16th hole	180	250
8th hole	310	340	17th hole	360	245
9th hole	288	245	18th hole	480	256

Seven miles from Edinburgh are two 18 hole golf courses on rolling heathland, with magnificent trees dividing up the holes.

The two courses were laid out by James Braid in 1927 under the new name of Dalmahoy – it was the Old Cramond Brig Golf Club from 1908 – and it is a tribute to his planning that no more than minor changes have since been made. The turf on these parkland courses is springy and clean and there are extensive views from the course to Arthur's Seat and Edinburgh Castle.

The clubhouse was formerly the ancestral home of the Earls of Morton, and the three-storied building is a superb example of fine Georgian architecture, spacious and dignified.

I played at the official opening of the East Course – the larger and tougher of the two courses – in 1929, with James Braid. The 6677 yard course is difficult to score low on. Several big events have since been played at Dalmahoy, for the club is conveniently situated to attract a large gathering of keen Edinburgh golfers.

Alex M. Fox, professional, writes:

I have been professional here for the last eleven years and have two assistants to cope with the 1000 members. The club, which lies some eight miles west of Edinburgh on the A71, has everything to commend it to visitors. Its two circuits, set in beautiful wooded country, provide the golfer with all the best features of parkland courses, but at the same time offer a stern though not fierce test of golfing ability.

Dalmahoy has always been a popular venue for local events but it is now rapidly gaining wider fame and has, in recent years, staged the British Boys' Open Championship and the British Girls' Stroke Play Championship, and it became a national tournament venue in 1962 when the first ever Senior Service £8000 Tournament was held here.

I think, without any doubt, that the 7th on the East course is the toughest hole. It is the show hole of the course, 430 yards long. Even the 'tiger' will find here that a long drive and a powerful second shot over the dip are called for if he is to get home in two to a green built up on a lefthand slope, with a bunker cutting into the left corner and another short on the right.

Club members include Findlay Black, a Scottish International and four times Dalmahoy Club Champion. Bernard Gallagher took over the championship for two years and has now, of course, turned professional.

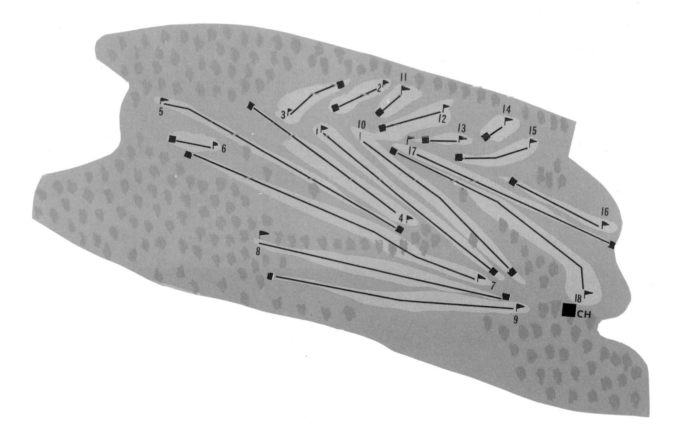

Troon Golf Course

Craigend Road, Troon, Ayrshire, Scotland

Tel: Troon 170

Secretary: A. Sweet

Nearest station: Troon — ¾ mile

Hotels: Marine Hotel, Troon;
Sun Court Hotel, Troon.

Visitors' fees:

Old Course: Weekdays 25/– per day;
Weekends 40/– per day;
Weekly ticket 70/–, excluding
Saturdays and Sundays.

Portland Course: Weekdays 20/– per day;
Weekends 40/– per day;
Weekly ticket 60/–, excluding
Saturdays and Sundays.

Length of Old Course
18 holes, 6720 yards

	yards		yards
1st hole	360	10th hole	395
2nd hole	370	11th hole	430
3rd hole	380	12th hole	455
4th hole	530	13th hole	400
5th hole	195	14th hole	175
6th hole	550	15th hole	440
7th hole	385	16th hole	540
8th hole	125	17th hole	215
9th hole	400	18th hole	375

No other corner, even in Scotland, offers such a varied feast of golf as you find in the ten miles of shore between Irvine and Ayr. Here are nearly a dozen courses of first-class tournament standard, among them Troon, which has been the scene of the Open and Amateur Championships many times, as well as staging many other noble golfing events.

Troon, an 'out-and-back' layout on coastal link land, had at one time both the longest and the shortest holes of any of the great courses: the 580-yard 6th, and the 125-yard 8th, which is still called the 'Postage Stamp' because that is just about as big as it looks from the elevated tee.

Despite its age the turf at Troon mysteriously retains its clean seaside texture, and the greens are firm – unlike the average 'puddings' of today – and somehow do not collect the ball.

Golf historians will find plenty to interest them in the clubhouse. As well as some magnificent silver, Troon possess what they claim to be the oldest set of golf clubs in existence, believed to date from the time of the Stuart kings.

I would list the 11th hole on the Old Course at Troon as being one of the world's most difficult golf holes, if not the toughest 485 yards of golf on earth.

History has been made on this course. Walter Hagen lost the 1923 Open Championship with a 5 at the Postage Stamp. P. B. 'Laddie' Lucas, our great long-driving lefthanded amateur, once cut his drive, with a helping wind from the sea, right into the grounds of the charming Marine Hotel which is situated on the 18th fairway: quite a slice! Bobby Locke, who won the 1959 Open there – a repeat win – did a record score of 279 with a 5 at the short 5th hole. Arthur Havers won the 1923 Open Championship here in his 23rd year and J. L. C. Jenkins, a local member, was Amateur Champion in 1914.

Visitors are welcome on weekdays to this golfer's paradise.

W. J. Henderson, professional, writes:
Troon Golf Club was founded in 1878 and we now have two courses, as well as a children's course and a good practice ground.
The greens are full of subtle borrows, not large, and the bunkers have a big catchment area.
The most difficult hole is the 11th on the Old Course, where the tee shot line is between a steep rough sandhill and a big patch of whins and has the green touching the wall of the railway line. Jack Nicklaus ruined his Open chances with a 10 at this hole in 1962.

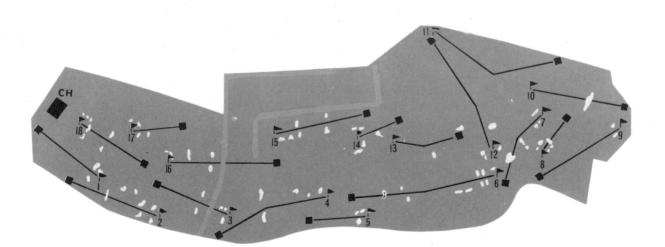

Blairgowrie Golf Club

Rosemount, Blairgowrie, Perthshire, Scotland

Tel: 116 (Professional)
     384 (Clubhouse)
     594 (Starter)

Secretary: R. C. Malcolm

Bus service from Perth and Dundee

Hotel: Royal Hotel, Blairgowrie

Course record: Professional, 69 by Brian Huggett
                  Amateur, 70 by D. A. Steven
                  and G. C. Mitchell

Visitors' fees: Weekdays 15/– per round,
              20/- per day;

              Weekends and Wednesdays
              20/– per round, 30/– per day;

              Weekly ticket £4.

18 holes, 6733 yards

	yards		yards
1st hole	450	10th hole	428
2nd hole	339	11th hole	510
3rd hole	226	12th hole	291
4th hole	440	13th hole	407
5th hole	541	14th hole	517
6th hole	167	15th hole	134
7th hole	330	16th hole	483
8th hole	548	17th hole	170
9th hole	392	18th hole	400

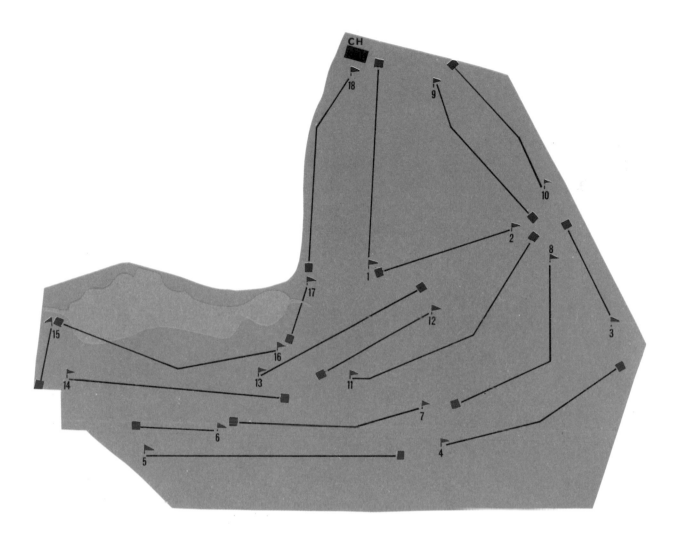

Rosemount, as the Blairgowrie Golf Club is generally known, is considered to be Scotland's greatest inland course. It is labelled a man's course, though it has no severe carries for ladies as the par fours are great.

The course, with no blind holes and no hills to climb, has over half the holes as doglegs, which makes the placing of the tee shot a 'must' to score easily. The fine turf makes easy walking.

The drive across the corner of the Black Loch at the 16th hole – where a golfer can easily hook into trouble – is one of Rosemount's most spectacular tee shots.

Gordon Kinnoch, professional, writes:

This golf club was formed in 1889 with a nine-hole course. It was eventually extended to eighteen holes, designed by James Braid.

The course lies in a setting of birch and pine trees, with the rough entirely of heather. The greens are large and undulating and as each hole is completely separated from its neighbour there is an atmosphere of seclusion and privacy as one plays this course. Visitors are struck, too, by the number and amazing variety of wild life: pheasants, partridges, squirrels, buck and, in the winter, geese by the thousand.

Probably the toughest hole is the 16th, a dogleg left over the edge of a loch with an out-of-bounds on the left: a narrow entrance to the green calls for a very accurate second shot.

Nairn Golf Club

Nairn, Nairnshire, Scotland

Tel: Nairn 3208

Secretary: E. J. Stone

Nearest station: Nairn — 1 mile

Hotels: many in Nairn

Course record: Professional, 65 by G. W. McIntosh
Amateur, 68 by D. M. Bowrie

Visitors' fees: Championship Course 12/6 per round,
20/– per day;
Newton Course 5/– per round.

Championship Course: 18 holes, 6429 yards

	yards		yards
1st hole	400	10th hole	504
2nd hole	456	11th hole	156
3rd hole	363	12th hole	450
4th hole	145	13th hole	435
5th hole	379	14th hole	200
6th hole	176	15th hole	311
7th hole	500	16th hole	426
8th hole	330	17th hole	365
9th hole	330	18th hole	503

Nairn Golf Club occupies a wonderful position along the shores of the Moray Firth. One is never out of sight of the sea on this course, indeed at the first seven holes it forms a natural boundary and many have been the balls mourned therein! But the view, with its ever-changing hues of Mediterranean intensity, is still a source of endless pleasure to visitors and locals alike. Standing on the first tee a player may take his line on one of the peaks in the Attadale Forest, a range of hills over 3500 feet and eighty miles away; then he can turn his head to see a vista of firth, mountains and foothills stretching far to the north.

I helped to launch the first Nairn Golf Week. Now every year nearly three hundred golfers go to Nairn in the early spring for a week's holiday which includes free tuition daily. This innovation really gives the summer season a great send-off.

As well as the Championship Course, Nairn also boasts the Newton Course, a nine-hole course very popular with the ladies and the children, and an extensive practice ground where, on Saturday mornings, Gregor McIntosh gives Golf Foundation lessons to twenty or more schoolchildren.

I love Nairn – to golf there is a real treat for every class of player.

Gregor McIntosh, professional, writes:

Nairn Golf Club was founded in 1887 and was first laid out by Archie Simpson of Aberdeen. All the fairways – except the 13th, 14th and 15th – run east and west amid whin and broom, ablaze in early summer, and heather, a glorious purple later in the year. The 5th hole, where the sea has encroached a little, requires a drive partly over the sea when the wind is in the north, making this one of the finest holes on the course, where a steady nerve is needed to place the drive to the ideal position to reach the green in 2. This was the favourite hole of the late James Braid, my old master and mentor, who advised on alterations from time to time and who knew just where to place a cunning bunker.

This fine championship course of 6429 yards, par 71, has staged many important events over the years. Here Jessie Valentine, now an established member of the Golf Week team, twice won the Scottish Ladies' title. Here the Scottish Amateurs and Professionals have battled, producing such champions as Ronnie Shade, John Panton and Eric Brown. Nairn's own most distinguished golfer is David Blair, Walker Cup player and Scottish Champion.

In recent years the Golf Week in May has brought an increasing number of enthusiasts to Nairn, some of whom return year after year for instructions from our team of well-known professionals, originally led by Henry Cotton and now in the capable hands of Dai Rees and six others, including myself. The programme includes competitions, films and exhibitions and, of course, endless talk of golf, golf, and still more golf!

My lowest score on the course is 62 – achieved on two successive days – and I hold the professional record of 65. My eclectic score is 37 – two at every hole except the 7th and no holes in one!

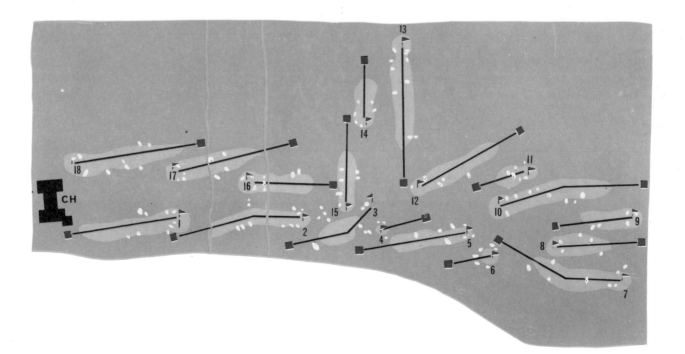

Royal St. David's Golf Club

Harlech, Merioneth, North Wales

Tel: Harlech 203

Secretary: H. Warburton
Tel: Harlech 361

Nearest station: Harlech — $\frac{1}{4}$ mile

Nearest hotel: St. David's Hotel, Harlech

Course record: Amateur 66 by J. L. Morgan
Professional 66 by J. L. Black

Visitors' fees: 1st April to 31st October: Weekends 30/– per day; 12/6 per round. Weekdays 1st November to 31st March: 20/– per day. Weekends: 20/– per day; Weekdays 12/6 per day. All fees halved for visitors playing with a member.

18 holes, 6282 yards

	yards		yards
1st hole	440	10th hole	424
2nd hole	340	11th hole	125
3rd hole	460	12th hole	425
4th hole	166	13th hole	448
5th hole	379	14th hole	211
6th hole	367	15th hole	417
7th hole	447	16th hole	354
8th hole	487	17th hole	421
9th hole	170	18th hole	201

The low-lying sheep-grazing land below the walls of Harlech Castle, between the shoreline and this famous fortress, was a 'natural' for a seaside golf links, and in due course one was built there. The architects skilfully laid out the course following the contours of the dunes and hillocks, consequently no two fairways run parallel to one another.

It was the year 1894 that saw the beginning of Harlech's modern history as a golf course. In 1912 it became Royal St. David's and, in 1935, the Duke of Windsor, when Prince of Wales, was Captain of the club and came to 'play himself in'.

The background view on the land side of this links is of Snowdon and the mountain range, with Edward I's Harlech Castle on the low hill in the foreground: grandiose scenery. On the sides of the fairways, tough rushes and dog roses punish those who err. There is only one starting point on this 6606 yard course.

Royal St. David's is a favourite course with the ladies, and many championships have been played there and will surely be played there in the future.

John L. Morgan holds the amateur course record with a 66. "I have done a 66, with a one at the ninth," says professional Jimmy Black modestly, as though a hole in one was scarcely worth a mention.

I have only played at Harlech once, and then it rained so pitilessly that we could hardly finish the game. My impression remains of a flat, bungalow-style clubhouse and a row of white railings lying beneath the dark green of the bushes and trees of the precipitous hillside, on the top of which the famous old castle, as Tom Scott says "stands broody sentinel over the surrounding countryside".

This is a golfing paradise really worth a visit, far from the smoke and the soot, the bustle and worry of modern city life.

J. L. Black, professional, writes:

This is a very good links with large, undulating greens, where the game can be thoroughly enjoyed by both 'tiger' and 'rabbit'. I would say that it is a very fair test of golf, indeed a good test when the wind blows a bit from the south west. The condition of the greens is always excellent, thanks to a most conscientious ground staff who all play and understand the game.

I think the 15th is the best hole on the course. It is a very natural, slightly dogleg right through the sandhills. The last five holes are good ones; although the last hole is a par 3 it is still a good test of golf.

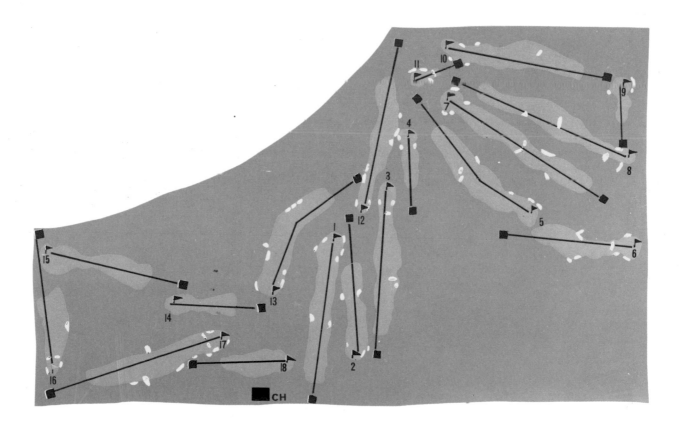

Royal Porthcawl Golf Club

Porthcawl, Glamorgan, Wales

Tel: Porthcawl 2251

Secretary: Major A. V. Norris, M.B.E.
Tel: Porthcawl 3847

Nearest station: Bridgend

Hotels: Esplanade Hotel, Porthcawl;
Seabank Hotel, Porthcawl

Visitors' fees: Weekdays 20/– per day
Weekends 25/– per day
Weekly tickets £4
Fortnightly tickets £6

18 holes, 6402 yards

	yards		yards
1st hole	330	10th hole	335
2nd hole	425	11th hole	188
3rd hole	384	12th hole	459
4th hole	186	13th hole	417
5th hole	460	14th hole	154
6th hole	394	15th hole	419
7th hole	125	16th hole	422
8th hole	445	17th hole	500
9th hole	369	18th hole	390

Right on the shores of the Bristol Channel lies the Royal Porthcawl Golf Club, another wonderful course in the championship class, with 6700 yards of exacting golf to master.

It is one of the select band of clubs with their diamond jubilees behind them. The construction of the course began in 1891 when professional Charles Gibson – from Westward Ho, just across the Channel – plotted out 9 holes. Nine more holes were added in 1895 and three years later the original nine were abandoned and the present course laid out. There have not been a great number of alterations since then, although Tom Simpson made some in 1934 and so did C. K. Cotton in 1950. The present course is, therefore, a bit of a composite job. But, except that it is another 'out and back', it could hardly be improved, for there are a number of dangerous holes where anything can happen. The enjoyment of the round is greatly enhanced by the magnificent view of the Channel at every hole.

I agree with Wally Gould on his choice of the 5th as the toughest hole. I know that I was always pleased to see my second shot stay in play on the uphill run of the fairway to that elevated green. The 374 yards 9th hole is stroke 1 on the card. The sloping green is the hardest part of this hole.

One of my best memories of golfing in South Wales is the drive at the 330 yards opening hole, for a decent hook sends the ball right on to the beach. I did a 66 over the course in 1931, which Percy Alliss beat by a stroke in the same event.

In 1909, the club became Royal Porthcawl and one of the many interesting souvenirs in the clubhouse is the full length picture of the Duke of Windsor as Prince of Wales.

Wally Gould, professional, writes:

Royal Porthcawl has been described as the best links in Wales and I think the claim is amply justified. It is a typical seaside links, with sandy subsoil which plays in dry condition for the twelve months of the year. The course is reasonably undulating, but quite easy to walk.

I came to Royal Porthcawl in 1927 as assistant to J. G. Hutcheson. He served the club for fifty years and I became his successor in 1948.

I would consider the 489 yard 5th hole to be the toughest, with the out-of-bounds boundary touching the edge of the green all along the left side. Many cards are spoiled here.

Most of the famous golfers have played this course during their careers. Tournaments held here include the British Amateur Championship, the British Ladies' Championship, the Men's and Ladies' International, the Dunlop Masters Tournament and the Curtis Cup.

We have two adequate practice areas, one with a bunkered green of 150 yards.

Killarney Golf Club

Mahony's Point, Killarney, County Kerry, Ireland

Tel: Killarney 34

Secretary: Captain D. D. O'Connell

Nearest station: Killarney — 3 miles

Hotels: Arbutus Hotel, Killarney;
Castlerosse Hotel, Killarney,
and other shareholding hotels.

Course record: Amateur, 70 by J. Carr
Professional, 66 by M. Guerin

Visitors' fees: 17/6 per day

18 holes, 6353 yards

	yards		yards
1st hole	340	10th hole	384
2nd hole	425	11th hole	157
3rd hole	424	12th hole	359
4th hole	390	13th hole	478
5th hole	345	14th hole	378
6th hole	157	15th hole	252
7th hole	480	16th hole	480
8th hole	434	17th hole	366
9th hole	322	18th hole	182

Golf was being played at Killarney in 1891, but the present Killarney Golf Course was designed by Sir Guy Campbell Bt. and Lord Castleross, later Earl of Kenmore, and opened in 1940. It is a very fine, modern course, 6714 yards from the back tees.

The beauties of Killarney have been extolled in song and verse throughout the world, and no visitor ever leaves disappointed. Three holes border on the lake and they are, as can be imagined, spectacular. The 182 yard 18th hole, across the water to the front of the clubhouse on Mahoney's Point, is glorious.

The photogenic qualities of the area attract many American television companies, who come to film and stay to play golf. Mike Souchak (70) beat Bobby Cole (72) in one game, and Joe Carr and Al Geiberger halved in one of Shell's Wonderful World of Golf. In an unofficial match with Bing Crosby, professional Tony Coveney had a best score of 66.

One of the great characters at Killarney is Dr. Billy O'Sullivan, an Irish international golfer for twenty years and the popular local 'Doc'.

Two of Ireland's amateur golfing heroes are Honorary Members of the club: Joe Carr and Jimmy Bruen, both 'Kings of Swat' in their day. They both think the world of Killarney . . . so will you all!

Tony Coveney, club professional and former assistant to Henry Cotton, writes:

Killarney is a lakeside, sandy course of
championship quality, with turf like Gleneagles.
Plans are at present under discussion for a new 18 hole
championship course on an additional 110 acres,
which will intersect the present course and have three
lakeside holes, making two starting points at the clubhouse.
The toughest hole is, in my opinion, the 13th,
of 478 yards. Here, the good player
is trying to make a four-elevated green, surrounded
by bunkers, the green falling away on all sides; to do this
he must hit the middle of the green and hold.
Many members, however, consider
that the 18th presents even more difficulty.
The lake lies on the right hand side of this
hole and it is bordered by bushes on the left, a
par three measuring 182 yards from medal tees.
The average golfer is a slicer and many balls
end up at the bottom of the lake.
There is a complete fairway of 300 yards by 100
yards as a practice hole, with green and bunker.
Future events to be played at Killarney include
the Irish Ladies' Championship in 1970
and the European Amateur Team Championship in 1973.

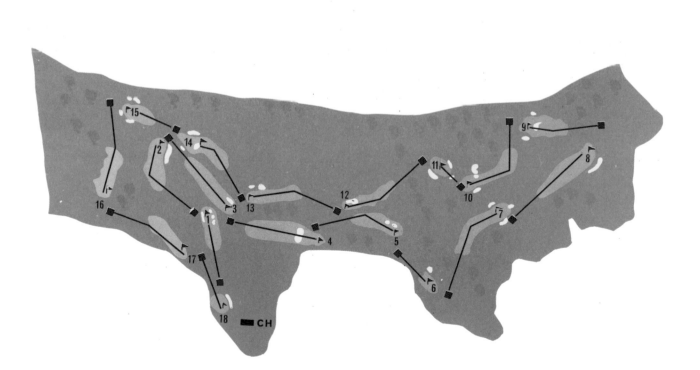

Portmarnock Golf Club

Portmarnock, County Dublin, Ireland

Tel: Dublin 323050
Secretary: R. H. Buck
Nearest station: Portmarnock — 2 miles
Nearest hotel: Marine Hotel, Sutton
Course record: Professional, 66 by Christy O'Connor
Visitors' fees: Weekdays 25/- per day
(10/- with member);

Weekends 30/- per day
(20/- with member).

Visitors must be introduced by a
member or the secretary of the club.

18 holes, 7053 yards

	yards		yards
1st hole	338	10th hole	380
2nd hole	368	11th hole	445
3rd hole	388	12th hole	144
4th hole	460	13th hole	565
5th hole	407	14th hole	385
6th hole	586	15th hole	192
7th hole	180	16th hole	527
8th hole	370	17th hole	466
9th hole	444	18th hole	403

This is one of the world's great golf courses, surrounded on three sides by water and with the usual sandhills and bushes, very rough grass and dog roses off the fairways. Situated on the coast ten miles north of Dublin, it provides 7053 yards of testing, but wholly enjoyable, golf.

The course dates from 1893. Early golfers, travelling home after their round of golf, had to cross from the point of the peninsula where the course is located over to the mainland. They crossed in boats or sometimes, at low tide, in horses and carts, although often floor deep in water.

Portmarnock has been host to many of golf's major events including the British Amateur Open Championship, the Dunlop Masters and the Canada Cup. The present professional Harry Bradshaw is one of the most interesting and natural golfers ever to stride a course.

I think that the 527-yard 16th hole is the best hole of this length that I have ever played: a dogleg to the right, usually against the prevailing northwest wind and with bunkers strategically positioned to catch even the wary player. It could go in any list of the world's 18 great holes.

There are no bad holes at Portmarnock, but the short 7th, 180 yards, is hard to stay on at times and has been criticised.

I first played at Portmarnock in 1927 – in the hickory-shafted days – when I was runner-up in the Irish Open, beaten by George Duncan's fabulous 74 in the first round. This round, played in a gale force wind, included – alas for me! – a kind bounce off a spectator's forehead to the front of the 18th green, from a second shot which was right out of bounds prior to the impact. George got a 4, it could have been a 6 or a 7!

My outstanding memory of Portmarnock is driving off the first tee at high tide with the water lapping against the side of the tee.

Harry Bradshaw, professional, writes:
Our greens are fair and always well kept, well watered and holding. We have two big practice areas, each over 400 yards long.

I would consider the 17th to be our toughest hole. It is a par 4, 466 yards long, a narrow tee shot through flanking bunkers, and for the second shot the gap between sand traps to the green is only from 15 to 18 yards wide.

I have done a 64 on the course, beginning with five threes and getting out in 30. The official record is 66 by Christy O'Connor, and Joe Carr and Jimmy Bruen have had 67s.

Portmarnock provides a good game of golf and has been enjoyed by many of the famous, including Bob Hope, Bing Crosby and Danny Kaye.

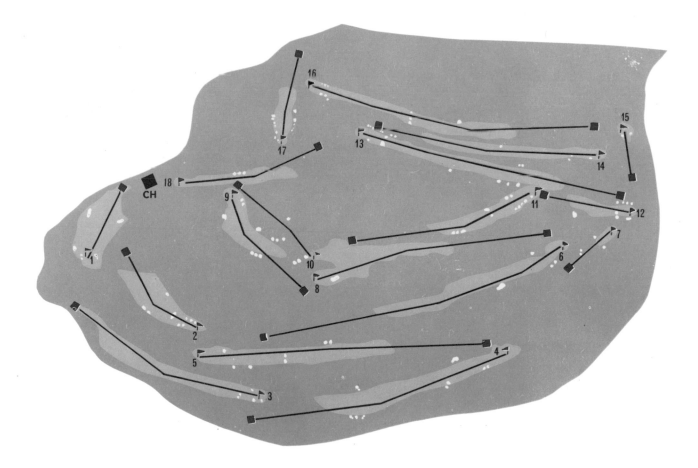

La Moye Golf Club

La Moye, St. Brelade, Jersey

Tel: 42701

Secretary: D. V. Mackay, D.S.O., T.D.

Bus service from St. Helier

Hotels: Bay Hotel, St. Brelade's Bay;
Hotel L'Horizon, St. Brelade's Bay.

Course record: 63 by P. Allis, G. M. Hunt
and A. Jacklin

Visitors' fees: Weekdays 30/– per day
(10/– with member);
Weekly tickets £5; Monthly tickets £15.

18 holes, 6310 yards

	yards		yards
1st hole	155	10th hole	345
2nd hole	435	11th hole	390
3rd hole	410	12th hole	500
4th hole	415	13th hole	455
5th hole	145	14th hole	505
6th hole	320	15th hole	175
7th hole	340	16th hole	425
8th hole	165	17th hole	380
9th hole	485	18th hole	265

One of two splendid courses on the island of Jersey in the Channel Islands, La Moye Golf Club lies on sandy ground some 250 feet above sea level, overlooking the wide sweep of St. Ouen's Bay. It must be the highest links type course in our islands and it certainly gets all the wind that is going, for there is no protection on this promontory on which it is located. The roof of the new clubhouse blew off in the winter of 1967.

La Moye was founded in 1902. The old course at Grouville – home of Harry and Tom Vardon – was getting crowded, so George Boomber, then headmaster of La Moye School, laid out the holes of this new course. Aubrey and Percy Boomber, sons of the founder, both became professionals and made their names in the golfing world. Aubrey served at the St. Cloud Club in Paris and won the French Open Championship several times.

This is an ideal holiday course. The views are unique and although the course is comparatively short it is an exacting test of golf, local knowledge being a decided advantage here.

Arthur Miner, club professional, writes:

This is a links type course, set in among the sandhills, and the scene from the clubhouse is unrivalled. The putting greens are always in beautiful condition, well watered and holding.

Our course was redesigned last winter by Henry Cotton and the new 14th and 15th are both great golf holes; of the two, in my opinion, the 15th stands out as probably the best short hole in the Channel Islands. It is played from an elevated tee to a built-up green 175 yards away, and one must hit the green to ensure a par, as it is very cleverly bunkered.

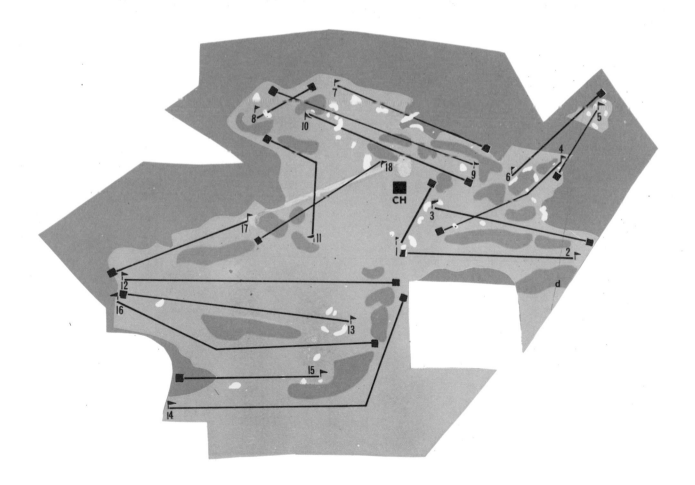

Castletown Golf Links Hotel

Fort Island, Castletown, Isle of Man

Tel: Castletown 2201
Situated 3 miles from Ronaldsway Airport
Hotel: Castletown Golf Links Hotel
Visitors' fees: 10/– per day, 40/– per week

18 holes, 6947 yards

	yards		yards
1st hole	295	10th hole	577
2nd hole	405	11th hole	170
3rd hole	565	12th hole	373
4th hole	395	13th hole	358
5th hole	506	14th hole	460
6th hole	135	15th hole	382
7th hole	390	16th hole	195
8th hole	445	17th hole	467
9th hole	380	18th hole	449

The original Derby was run in the Isle of Man and the racecourse is now the tenth hole of the Castletown Golf Links. It is also claimed that the course has been the scene of ancient battles and that the Vikings landed here. But today this picturesque peninsula is given over to more friendly battles. The struggle now is mainly between man and nature in a splendid test of golf.

The situation of this triangular course is breathtaking, with sea on three sides and marvellous vistas to enjoy at every hole. Another feature of the course is the fact that several of the holes are separated from the sea by formations of rocks which can be regarded by the golfer as attractive or a complete nuisance, depending on how well he overcomes these natural obstacles.

This modern post-war course was designed by Mackenzie Ross and includes three holes of 565, 577 and 506 yards.

The long 3rd hole – 565 yards from the back tee – is a great test, in fact a really big hole in every sense. Another splendid hole is the 445 yard 8th which, like the famous hole at St. Andrews, is named 'The Road'. The tee is set high and there is little room for error here. The beach is not far away, separated from the course by the road from which this hole got its name. If the drive demands considerable accuracy so does the second shot, which has to be played over a cross-bunker to a green cut out of the rising ground on the left, with the road and the beach lying on the right. Even the tigers are glad to get away from this hole with a five.

Murray C. Crowe, professional, writes:

Castletown golf course is situated on a peninsula so that as well as providing magnificent views for the player to enjoy it has the added stimulus of very variable wind conditions. Holes which can be played with the wind against you in the morning can take on an entirely different character in the afternoon and then again can change for the few holes which are played in the evening. Golf can never be dull at Castletown.

One of the most difficult holes is the 7th from the tiger tee, which is also the only hole on the course where you play with your back to the sea. This is a dogleg, taking a good drive to reach the fairway over the gorse and heather, and then demanding a well-hit shot to a small green with a narrow entrance and two well-placed bunkers. A bunker at the back of this green will often catch the unwary.

Another great hole is the short 11th which, depending on the wind, can be either a 7 iron or a 3 wood.

The last three holes – pars 3, 4 and 4 – are the greatest test. The average golfer who is playing to his handicap and succeeds in getting par figures at these holes will finish his round of golf with a distinct sense of achievement.

Guide to courses

England
1 Wentworth
2 Royal Lytham St Annes
3 Ipswich
4 Royal Blackheath
5 Walton Heath
6 Royal St Georges
7 Royal Mid-Surrey
8 Manor House
9 West Hill
10 Sunningdale
11 Royal Liverpool
12 Royal Cinque Ports
13 Worplesdon
14 Little Aston
15 Royal Wimbledon
16 Crowborough Beacon
17 Lindrick
18 Thorpe Hall
19 Addington
20 Denham
21 Royal Birkdale
22 Royal Ashdown Forest
23 Alwoodley
24 Moor Park
25 Woodhall Spa
26 Burnham and Berrow
27 Royal North Devon
28 Parkstone
29 Fulwell
30 West Sussex
31 West Cornwall
32 Moortown
33 Hunstanton
34 Temple
35 Ashridge
36 Sandy Lodge
37 Notts
38 Formby
39 Yelverton
40 Coombe Hill
41 Hankley Common
42 Liphook

Scotland
43 St Andrews
44 Gleneagles
45 Muirfield
46 Carnoustie
47 Turnberry
48 Dalmahoy
49 Troon
50 Blairgowrie
51 Nairn

Wales
52 Royal St David's
53 Royal Porthcawl

Ireland
54 Killarney
55 Portmarnock

Jersey
56 La Moye

Isle of Man
57 Castletown

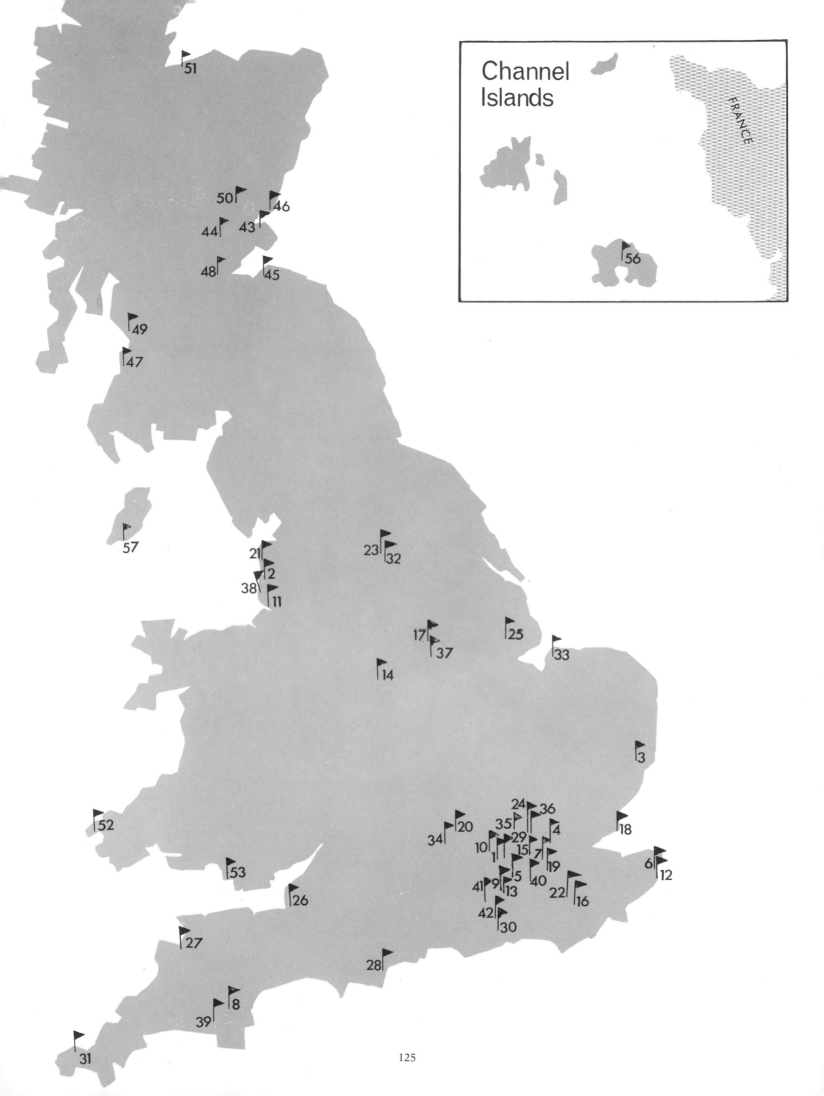

Channel
Islands

FRANCE